# The Kindest People
# Who Do Good Deeds: Volume 1
### David Bruce

# The Kindest People Who Do Good Deeds: Volume 1

**Kindest People Who Do Good Deeds, Volume 1**

David Bruce

Published by David Bruce, 2022.

While every precaution has been taken in the preparation of this book, the publisher assumes no responsibility for errors or omissions, or for damages resulting from the use of the information contained herein.

THE KINDEST PEOPLE WHO DO GOOD DEEDS: VOLUME 1

**First edition. August 23, 2022.**

Copyright © 2022 David Bruce.

ISBN: 979-8201071752

Written by David Bruce.

# Table of Contents

# Dedication

**Dedicated to Carl Eugene Bruce and Josephine Saturday Bruce**

My father, Carl Eugene Bruce, died on 24 October 2013. He used to work for Ohio Power, and at one time, his job was to shut off the electricity of people who had not paid their bills. He sometimes would find a home with an impoverished mother and some children. Instead of shutting off their electricity, he would tell the mother that she needed to pay her bill or soon her electricity would be shut off. He would write on a form that no one was home when he stopped by because if no one was home he did not have to shut off their electricity.

The best good deed that anyone ever did for my father occurred after a storm that knocked down many power lines. He and other linemen worked long hours and got wet and cold. Their feet were freezing because water got into their boots and soaked their socks. Fortunately, a kind woman gave my father and the other linemen dry socks to wear.

My mother, Josephine Saturday Bruce, died on 14 June 2003. She used to work at a store that sold clothing. One day, an impoverished mother with a baby clothed in rags walked into the store and started shoplifting in an interesting way: The mother took the rags off her baby and dressed the infant in new clothing. My mother knew that this mother could not afford to buy the clothing, but she helped the mother dress her baby and then she watched as the mother walked out of the store without paying.

***

The doing of good deeds is important. As a free person, you can choose to live your life as a good person or as a bad person. To be a good person, do good deeds. To be a bad person, do bad deeds. If you do good deeds, you will become good. If you do bad deeds, you will become bad. To become the person you want to be, act as if you already are that kind of person. Each of us chooses what kind of person we will become. To become a good person, do the things a good person does. To become a bad person, do the things a bad person does. The opportunity to take action to become the kind of person you want to be is yours.

Human beings have free will. According to the Babylonian Niddah 16b, whenever a baby is to be conceived, the Lailah (angel in charge of contraception) takes the drop of semen that will result in the conception and asks God, "Sovereign of the Universe, what is going to be the fate of this drop? Will it develop into a robust or into a weak person? An intelligent or a stupid person? A wealthy or a poor person?" The Lailah asks all these questions, but it does not ask, "Will it develop into a righteous or a wicked person?" The answer to that question lies in the decisions to be freely made by the human being that is the result of the conception.

A Buddhist monk visiting a class wrote this on the chalkboard: "EVERYONE WANTS TO SAVE THE WORLD, BUT NO ONE WANTS TO HELP MOM DO THE DISHES." The students laughed, but the monk then said, "Statistically, it's highly unlikely that any of you will ever have the opportunity to run into a burning orphanage and rescue an infant. But, in the smallest gesture of kindness — a warm smile, holding the door for the person behind you, shoveling the driveway of the elderly person next door — you have committed an act of immeasurable profundity, because to each of us, our life is our universe."

In her book titled *I Have Chosen to Stay and Fight*, comedian Margaret Cho writes, "I believe that we get complimentary snack-size portions of the afterlife, and we all receive them in a different way." For Ms. Cho, many of her snack-size portions of the afterlife come in hip hop music. Other people get different snack-size portions of the afterlife, and we all must be on the lookout for them when they come our way. And perhaps doing good deeds and experiencing good deeds are snack-size portions of the afterlife.

The Zen master Gisan was taking a bath. The water was too hot, so he asked a student to add some cold water to the bath. The student brought a bucket of cold water, added some cold water to the bath, and then threw the rest of the water on a rocky path. Gisan scolded the student: "Everything can be used. Why did you waste the rest of the water by pouring it on the path? There are some plants nearby which could have used the water. What right do you have to waste even a drop of water?" The student became enlightened and changed his name to Tekisui, which means "Drop of Water."

# INTRODUCTION

**Tipping the Balance—Either Way**

According to the Talmud, all of us ought to consider the world as being equally divided into good and evil. That way, we will regard our own actions as important. If we act evilly, we will tip the world onto the side of evil and all Humankind will suffer, but if we perform good deeds, we will tip the world onto the side of good, and all Humankind will benefit.

# Chapter 1: COMEDIANS

### "Don't A T'ing Like Dis Make Ya Feel Good?"

Comedians Jimmy Durante and Eddie Cantor were very giving of their time to good causes. On New Year's Day of 1943, Mr. Durante met Mr. Cantor while taking a walk. "Eddie," Mr. Durante said, "I'm just thinkin'. This must be a tough time for the guys over there in that hospital. Here it's New Year's Day, they're sick, some of 'em have amputations. What do ya say we go over and entertain?" The two comedians rehearsed for a short time, and then they entertained at the hospital from 10:30 a.m. to 5 p.m. Afterward, Mr. Durante said hoarsely to Mr. Cantor, "Eddie, tell me, don't a t'ing like dis make ya feel good?"

### Stranded in Kent, Ohio

In Kent, Ohio, early in his vaudeville days, W.C. Fields found himself stranded. (At this time, he was still being victimized by tour managers who would abscond with their performers' salaries.) He had six dollars, sold his coat for two dollars, and then went to the railroad station to inquire about the fare to New York. The railroad agent told him that it was just over $10. (Ten dollars in 1894 was the rough equivalent of over $200 in the year 2000.) "Well, I guess I'm stuck," Mr. Fields said. "I've got eight dollars." The agent asked if he was an entertainer, and on hearing that Mr. Fields was, he said, "People don't put much trust in you folks, do they?" (At this time, being an entertainer was about as low on the social scale as a person could be.) "We're used to it," Mr. Fields said. The agent then gave Mr. Fields $10 and said, "I've always wondered what there was to that story. When you get a little ahead, send this back." That rare act of kindness impressed Mr. Fields so much that he sat on a bench and cried. Two years later, Mr. Fields was finally able to repay the debt. On Christmas Eve, 1896, he sent $20 to the railroad agent ($10 was for "interest"), and then he stood in line at a free soup kitchen for a Christmas dinner. After Mr. Fields became a huge success, he looked up the agent, as did other famous show people who learned what the agent had done for Mr. Fields.

### Tennis Shoes and a Pink Umbrella

One book that Gilda Radner read and enjoyed was *Disturbances in the Dark* by Lynne Sharon Schwartz. The main female character in the book

remembers that when she was a young girl, she, her sister, and her parents would go to the beach. So that the two young girls would always be able to find the beach umbrella their parents were using, her father tied a pair of tennis shoes to the umbrella. The two young girls felt safe and protected when they saw the umbrella with the pair of shoes hanging from it. The night before Gilda underwent her first chemotherapy after being diagnosed with ovarian cancer, her husband, Gene Wilder, walked into her hospital room carrying a little pink umbrella to which he had tied some shoes.

**My Fellow Bums**

While living in New York City, comedian Bill Hicks was shocked by the number of homeless people he saw, and he always left home with change in his pockets to give to the homeless. He pointed out, "I could have been a bum. All it takes is the right girl, the right bar, and the right friends."

**Visiting the Wounded Troops**

Comedian Al Franken goes into Veterans Administration hospitals to meet the wounded troops. He thought that it would be very difficult, but he was amazed by how cheerful many of them—including a woman helicopter pilot who had lost most of her left leg and part of her right leg—are. He asked a man with one leg what had happened to him; the man replied, "I came in here for a vasectomy, and when I woke up my leg was gone." By the way, Mr. Franken says not to thank these wounded veterans for their service to the country—they imitate all the politicians who tell them that. Therefore, Mr. Franken uses humor. When he has a photograph taken with one of these veterans, he writes on the photo, "Thank you for getting grievously wounded."

**"Paid, and Thanks. Danny"**

When British comedian Danny La Rue asked fellow entertainer Larry Grayson to entertain at his club while he went on vacation for two weeks, he showed much kindness to Mr. Grayson. First, he showed him his own dressing room and asked if any alterations needed to be made. Of course, everything was excellent. During the first week of Mr. Grayson's vacation, Mr. Grayson ran up a rather high tab, but when he called for his bill so he could pay it off, he was surprised to be given a bill marked, "Paid, and thank you. Danny." The next time Mr. Grayson was asked what he wished to be served in his dressing room, he said, "Just a coffee, please," thinking that he would not run up his tab because Mr. La Rue would pay for it. However, when he was informed that this week he would have to pay his own bill, he ordered what he really wanted: a gin and tonic. At the end of the second week, Mr. Grayson again asked for his bill, and again it came to him marked, "Paid, and thank you. Danny." Mr. La Rue had known that Mr. Grayson would not order what he wanted and would not run up his bill the second week if he had thought that Mr. La Rue would pay it, so he had left orders for Mr. Grayson to be falsely told that the second week he would have to pay his own bill.

**Homeless, Coatless, and Penniless**

Before becoming a famous country comedian and star of *Hee Haw*, Archie Campbell was homeless, coatless, and penniless on a bitterly cold night in Knoxville, Tennessee. After getting thrown out of the bus station where he had fallen asleep, Mr. Campbell started walking in an unsuccessful effort to keep warm. Seeing an all-night restaurant, he went in and stood near a hot radiator. The owner, a Greek named Nick, asked him what he was doing. Mr. Campbell said that he lived nearby (a lie because he had no home), he had forgotten his coat (a lie because he had no coat), and he had dropped in to get warm (not a lie). Nick asked where he lived, and Mr. Campbell answered with the name of the first apartment complex he could think of. Apparently satisfied, Nick invited him to sit in a booth and get warm. Mr. Campbell fell asleep in a booth, and when he woke up, Nick set a huge, hot breakfast in front of him. Mr. Campbell explained that he couldn't pay for the meal, but Nick said he didn't have to—he knew that Mr. Campbell was homeless because he lived in the apartment complex that Mr. Campbell had named. After becoming rich and famous, Mr. Campbell made sure to stop in at that restaurant wherever he was in Knoxville.

**Comedian and Nurse**

Martha Raye was a wide-mouthed comedian who played an important role in Charlie Chaplin's 1947 black comedy, *Monsieur Verdoux*. She endeared herself—as did Bob Hope—by performing frequently for United States servicemen. In South Vietnam, her early training as a nurse's aide came in handy. She arrived on the morning of a day on which there was a big battle. When wounded soldiers started pouring into camp, she put on fatigues and worked as a nurse for 13 hours. After getting some sleep, she worked as a nurse again the next day. For this action, General William Childs Westmoreland recognized her services as both a comedian and a nurse.

### Cold Winters

In Toledo, Ohio, in the early part of the 20th century, a man named John Mockett ran a clothing store. Every winter, he saw impoverished kids on the street selling newspapers, and if they needed an overcoat, he would give them one. One of the boys to whom he gave an overcoat was Joe E. Brown, who later became a famous comedian.

### Branded a "Red"

John Henry Faulk was a humorist who seemed destined for the big time, but he was branded a "Red" during the Communist scare of the 1950s, so CBS Radio stopped running his show, *Johnny's Front Porch*. The famous journalist Ed Murrow mortgaged his house so that Mr. Faulk would be able to hire Louis Nizer, a famous attorney, in his fight for justice.

### Stage Time

Stand-up comedian Richard Belzer once came through for fellow stand-up comedian Judy Tenuta in a big way. Ms. Tenuta needed to audition for late-night talk show host David Letterman at the Improv, but she couldn't get stage time. An appearance on David Letterman's late-night talk show had enormous value in making a comedian's reputation, and she was desperate to find stage time so she could audition. Mr. Belzer allowed her to perform for 15 minutes before his act at Caroline's so she could do the audition there. At the time, Mr. Belzer didn't even know her.

### Heckling the Hecklers

Comedian Danny Thomas made a reputation in Chicago, and then he went to New York City to appear at Club Martinique. Several New York comics heard he was coming, so they decided to go to the nightclub and squelch the newcomer by heckling him. Because Mr. Thomas' type of humor involved the telling of long stories, heckling would destroy his act. Fortunately, Milton Berle was in the audience. Mr. Berle liked Mr. Thomas, and whenever a heckler started talking, it was Mr. Berle who put the heckler in his place with a comic insult. Very quickly, the hecklers left Mr. Thomas alone, and he went on to become a giant of comedy.

### "Do Dollar Bills Come That High?"

When Jamie Masada started The Laugh Factory in Los Angeles, he asked his friend Paul Mooney to emcee. Happy to help, Mr. Mooney did just that—and he brought Richard Pryor with him. Mr. Masada had made the vow that he would always pay any comedians who performed at his club, even if all he could afford was three or four dollars. Mr. Pryor, a gifted and moneyed and generous comedian, wouldn't take any money, but instead gave him a $100 bill, saying, "Good luck. You'll need this for your rent." Mr. Masada was shocked, in part because he didn't know that dollar bills came in denominations higher than a twenty. Hearing this, Mr. Pryor got a good laugh—and handed Mr. Masada four more $100 bills.

### A Gift for a Brother

Like many famous people who started out making little money, comedian Fred Allen was well aware of the price of consumables. He enjoyed smoking a certain cigar that cost 10 cents each, and each week he bought two boxes—one for himself, and one for his brother. When the price went up to 15 cents a cigar, he seriously considered not buying that brand but continued to buy two boxes a week. When the price went up to 20 cents a cigar, Mr. Allen felt that the price was too expensive, so he bought only one box of cigars each week—to send to his brother.

### A Weekly Check for $25

Gracie Allen had an aunt who was fairly well off until the stock market crash of 1929. When George Burns and Gracie Allen were just breaking into vaudeville, Aunt Clara used to send them a check for $25 each week, a habit she continued even when the comedy team of Burns and Allen was making thousands of dollars a week. In the stock market crash, Aunt Clara lost just about everything she had, but she never knew it, because Ms. Allen used to deposit enough money into Aunt Clara's checking account each month to cover all her expenses—including her weekly $25 check to Burns and Allen.

### Lost and Hungry

While in Colorado, comedian Henry Morgan and a friend were driving around, lost and hungry, when they spied a farmhouse with a decrepit sign saying "Restaurant" out in front. They stopped, ordered breakfast, and ate it, and then Mr. Morgan asked the old woman who had waited on them how much they owed. "Nothing," she answered, and then she explained that the farmhouse hadn't been a restaurant for 30 years. Mr. Morgan writes, "The old darling couldn't let a couple of nice kids starve."

### A Gang of Seven Tough Men

When African-American comedian Dick Gregory was just breaking into show business and making $30 a week, he took his girlfriend and her mother and siblings to a drive-in movie, spending every dime he had—and trying to keep that fact secret from everyone else. When the movie was over, snow had fallen, and his car and the other cars got stuck. A gang of seven tough men—all white—began pushing cars that were stuck, but they charged $5 for each push, and Mr. Gregory was broke. But he got out of the car, explained the situation to the men, and they pushed his car for free. One of the men even dropped a $5 bill in his lap.

**More Generosity in a Snowstorm**

African-American comedian Dick Gregory could be very generous. He once performed at the Village Gate in New York while a snowstorm was raging. Because of the snowstorm, only about 10 people were in the audience, and Art D'Lugoff, the owner of the club, was facing a big financial loss due to Mr. Gregory's salary. However, Mr. Gregory looked at Mr. D'Lugoff and said, "Don't worry, Art—this one's on me."

**A Rich Comedian**

Malcolm Scott was a British music-hall comedian who had the good fortune to be rich. Often, he used his money to perform good deeds. After completing his performance late at night, he would go to a poor quarter of town and seek a stall where people sold coffee and food. His habitual practice was to buy the entire contents of the stall and then hand out free coffee and food to the needy. Once, he noticed a small boy and small girl in a soup line on a very cold day—the girl was standing on the boy's cap to keep out the cold from the stones of the path. He immediately took them to a shelter and made arrangements for them to be taken care of.

**Comedic Charity**

As part of his act, comedian Jack Benny had a reputation for being cheap; in real life, he was generous—but in a funny way. Once he gave a million dollars to charity—then he pretended to faint. Jack Benny would also attend charity auctions—and raise the bidding one cent at a time. This made the other auction-goers laugh and put them in the mood to bid ever higher.

**"This is for Dessert"**

After Jack Benny declined to attend a fund-raising dinner with his friend Eddie Cantor, Mr. Cantor went alone. As the dinner was ending, an envelope was brought to Mr. Cantor. Inside was a signed blank check, with a note from Mr. Benny: "This is for dessert, Eddie. Fill in the amount. Love, Jack."

**Showing Kindness to a Remarried Divorced Woman**

Country comedian Jerry Clower's mother got divorced from her husband because he was an alcoholic who had abandoned his family. Despite the good reasons for the divorce, many people—including people in the church—shunned her because she was divorced. When she remarried, a neighbor who never set foot in the church and was considered a pretty rough character came by and gave the newly married couple a bushel of sweet potatoes for a wedding present, saying, "I hope y'all are happy. I'm digging my potatoes, and I don't have anything else to give you." This impressed Mr. Clower, who is a sincere Christian: "I thought it was interesting that a man who never went to church would be one of the few who was nice to my mama."

**"Everybody, Get Down!"**

Country comedian Jerry Clower has a lot of respect for Delta Airlines and its employees. One day, his daughter was flying Delta. She had to change planes at the Dallas/Fort Worth airport, and a crazed man with a gun grabbed a young boy and starting yelling and shooting the gun in the air. A Delta employee yelled, "Everybody, get down!" He then stood between the gunman and the passengers. Several other Delta employees came running up and locked arms with the first employee, forming a human barricade to protect the passengers—the only way the gunman could shoot the passengers behind the human barricade was to first shoot the Delta employees. (Fortunately, the gunman was overcome, and no one was hurt.)

**A Very Great Artist**

Charlie Chaplin, like many other rich and famous people in the days before such helping programs as Welfare and Social Security, dispensed pensions to friends and acquaintances who were aged and impoverished. When Mr. Chaplin was young, a magician used to entertain him on the streets of London. When the magician became aged and impoverished, he wrote Mr. Chaplin for help. Immediately, Mr. Chaplin put him on his pension list, saying, "He was a very great artist."

**Expensive Gifts**

Comedian Fanny Brice (famous for her Baby Snooks character) had a favorite friend from her Ziegfeld Follies days, Ann Pennington. Ms. Brice continued in show business and big bucks, but Ms. Pennington got out of show business. Ms. Brice enjoyed buying Penny expensive gifts, but she worried that Ms. Pennington would feel bad about accepting them. Ms. Brice solved her problem by buying Ms. Pennington expensive clothes, ripping out the brand-name labels, and sewing in the labels of a less expensive brand.

### Anonymous Tuition

Carol Burnett wanted to go to UCLA after she graduated from high school with good grades. Unfortunately, her family was poor and so there wasn't enough money for her to go. After all, tuition cost $42 (it was a long time ago), and books also cost money. One day Ms. Burnett went to the mailbox and found an envelope with no return address but with her name on it. She opened the envelope and found $50—even after becoming famous, she never discovered who had sent her the money. At UCLA, she began to study acting and later became rich and famous as a comedian.

### God has a Way of Compensating

While growing up, Geri Jewell wanted to be a comedian, but because she had cerebral palsy, no one gave her much chance of achieving her dream. She wrote TV comedian Carol Burnett and asked whether Ms. Burnett thought she could make her dream come true. Ms. Burnett wrote back, "I really admire your dedication in pursuing a career as a comedienne, and while no one can guarantee success, I would say you are on the right track by realizing your handicaps and assets. God has a way of compensating those who have been handicapped, Geri. Whether or not you turn 'pro' I know you will always enjoy good humor, and live life to its fullest. Don't give up. Get involved in acting in any capacity." Ms. Jewell did become a professional comedian, and she landed a recurring role on the TV series *Facts of Life*.

### Joking with the Dying

When Jim Backus, the voice of Mr. Magoo and a star of *Gilligan's Island*, lay dying, comedian Milton Berle stopped by and entertained him with corny jokes for two hours. When Mr. Berle left, he told his friend, "I hope you get better." Mr. Backus joked, "You, too."

### A Toothless Old Man

Comedian Fred Allen was an amazingly generous human being. One day, he ran into a toothless old man whom he had known in vaudeville, so he told him to see a dentist, get a set of false teeth, and have the bill sent to him. The old man was reluctant, but Mr. Allen said, "Go get some teeth, Irving—one of these days you might want to laugh at something."

**An Old 1934 Ford Pickup Truck**

While in high school, comedian Jay Leno bought an old 1934 Ford pickup truck. He worked hard to get it in shape, and his parents bought him new upholstery for it. One day, he slammed a truck door and shattered the window. Although he didn't have the money to replace the window, he continued to drive the car to school. While he was sitting in class one day, a big storm blew up and Jay looked at his car through the schoolroom window, knowing that the rain would ruin the upholstery. Suddenly, he saw his parents drive up and put plastic over the broken window to keep the rain out. His father had left work and picked up his mother so they could save Jay's upholstery. Right there in class, Jay started crying.

**Fire!**

Comedian Frank Fay exhibited coolness during a fire at the Schubert Theatre in New York. As smoke swirled around him, Mr. Fay walked out on stage and spoke calmly to the audience. He announced that there was a fire, but that he would personally press anyone's suit if it got wet from the hose of the firemen. Everyone laughed, no one panicked, and everyone got safely out of the theater.

# Chapter 2: SPORTS

**Food for a Hungry Family**

When Jackie Robinson was very young, his father abandoned the family. Therefore, his mother moved the family from Georgia to California, where she worked very long hours for not very much money. The family sometimes ate only two meals per day, and sometimes they would not have eaten at all if his mother had not brought home leftovers from her job as a housekeeper. Fortunately, other people helped the Robinsons. A baker did not keep his shop open on Sunday, so on Saturday afternoons he gave the Robinsons the leftover bread. A milkman also helped by occasionally giving the Robinsons extra milk. In 1924, Jackie and Willa Mae, his sister, often went to school hungry—so hungry they sometimes found it difficult to stand up. Their teachers—Bernie Gilbert and Beryl Haney—helped by bringing them sandwiches.

**Stopping Racial Abuse**

When Jackie Robinson became the first black man to play in baseball's major leagues in the 20th century, he was subjected to torrents of racist abuse from fans and opposing players. At one game, Mr. Robinson's fellow Brooklyn Dodgers teammate Pee Wee Reese, a white man, stopped the abuse. Mr. Robinson was standing at first base, and Mr. Reese walked over and put his arm around him.

**"I Don't Care if the Guy ... has Stripes"**

When Jackie Robinson broke the color barrier in major-league baseball, he made it possible for other African-American players to join the major leagues—and to start cashing some major-league checks. Willie Mays once said, "Every time I look in my pocketbook, I see Jackie Robinson." (Mr. Robinson had some help breaking the color barrier. Leo Durocher told the white players on the team in 1947, "I don't care if the guy is yellow or black or if he has stripes like a f**king zebra. I'm the manager of this team, and I say he plays.")

**A Superstar of Sport and a Scared Rookie**

In 1964, Rico Carty started playing baseball for the Braves. Mr. Carty came from the Dominican Republic, and manager Bobby Bragan wanted him to room with someone who would teach him English, so he asked for a volunteer.

Hank Aaron volunteered, greatly impressing Mr. Carty when he heard through a translator what the great home-run hitter had done. A superstar of sport had made a scared rookie feel welcome.

**"You Know You'll Never Get That Back, Don't You?"**

Baseball manager Larry Gilbert of the Southern Association was known for his many good deeds during the first half of the 20th century. Once, a man who had played baseball for him and who was almost always short of money got in a jam and asked him for a "loan" of $100—a lot of money back then. Mr. Gilbert gave him the money. Later, a friend of his told him, "You know you'll never get that back, don't you?" Mr. Gilbert replied, "That's all right. He played mighty good ball for me, better than I expected. Maybe I owe him a little something." In addition, a number of untalented young ballplayers showed up each spring to try out for his team and spent all their money without making the team. Mr. Gilbert always gave them railroad fare so they could get home.

**"If They Lose, I'll Walk Home"**

On 8 June 1989, Pittsburgh Pirates TV announcer Jim Rooker was so sure that the Pirates would end a 6-game losing streak after they opened up a 10-0 lead over the Philadelphia Phillies that he said that he would walk home all the way from Philadelphia to Pittsburgh if the Pirates lost the game. The Pirates did lose, 15-11. Mr. Rooker did walk home—not right away, but after the season ended. From October 5 to October 18, 1989, he walked the entire distance from Philadelphia to Pittsburgh, picking up donations for charity all the way.

**"Tracey is on Cloud Nine"**

In the 1981 World Series, the Dodgers played the Yankees. Retired Dodger pitcher Carl Erskine attended one of the games, where he talked to an old teammate, Clyde King, who now worked as a Yankee. Mr. Erskine mentioned that he knew a 12-year-old boy named Tracey Gustin, a Little League catcher who was a Yankee fan and who had terminal bone cancer. Of course, Mr. Erskine was hoping that one of the Yankees would give the boy a telephone call. Yankee star Reggie Jackson overheard the conversation and said, "Get the number, Clyde. I'll do it." Later, Mr. Erskine got a call from Tracey's mother, who told him, "Guess what happened. The Yankees called Tracey from Yankee Stadium just now—Bob Lemon, the manager, Catfish Hunter, Reggie Jackson, Goose Gossage, Yogi Berra, and Clyde King all talked to Tracey. ... Tracey is on cloud nine."

### "Keep It and Make Some Money"

Sal Durante caught the baseball Roger Maris hit to break Babe Ruth's single-season home-run record of 60. Mr. Durante, a nice guy, offered Mr. Maris the record-breaking baseball. However, Mr. Maris, also a nice guy, told him, "Keep it and make some money." Mr. Durante did, selling it for $5,000. The buyer, the owner of a restaurant, yet another nice guy, also threw in a couple of trips to the West Coast.

### "Hey, Pop!"

When baseball player Joe Garagiola's father was ill and dying, he watched his famous son speak on TV at a dinner in honor of Senator John F. Kennedy, who was running for President. Many, many VIPs were present, including former President Harry Truman. Joe knew that his father was dying, and he knew that his father would enjoy seeing him with all these VIPs, so he asked President Truman to stand beside him, and next he asked a Senator and a Governor to come and stand beside him. Finally, he put his arm around a couple of the VIPs, including Harry Truman, leaned toward the TV camera, and said, "Hey, Pop, I just want you to see who I'm hanging with." This made his father very happy and very proud.

### A 62-Year-Old Major League Pitcher

In 1968, at age 62, Satchel Paige was signed as a pitcher-coach by the Atlanta Braves for exactly 158 days. Why? The owner of the Braves, Bill Bartholomay, knew that Mr. Paige needed to work for exactly 158 days to be qualified for a pension.

### "You're Out of the Game!"

On the last day of the season, Frank Lary, a pitcher for Detroit, which wasn't going to play at all in the playoffs that year, wanted to go home on a 3 p.m. flight even though the game started at 2 p.m. Of course, he was expected to be at the game and stay there, even though he wasn't pitching, so he asked umpire Ed Runge for help. Umpires are often nice people, no matter what fans yell at a game, so Mr. Runge agreed to help. On the very first pitch of the game, Mr. Lary yelled, "Hey, Runge, what kind of a call is that?" Mr. Runge yelled back, "You're out of the game!"—and Mr. Lary made his flight with time to spare.

### My Sister Back in Kansas

Known for his fast balls, baseball player Walter Johnson was also known for being a gentleman. One day, a couple of people recognized him and talked to him for 20 minutes. His friend and teammate Joe Judge asked what they had been talking about. Mr. Johnson replied, "These men were telling me they knew my sister back in Kansas." Surprised, Mr. Judge said, "I never knew you had a sister." Mr. Johnson replied, "I don't."

**An Anonymous Good-Deed Doer**

Joan Joyce fielded and hit well as a softball player on the United States' best team—the Raybestos Brakettes—but she was not a pitcher. She could throw hard, but she had no control. Fortunately, one day a telephone lineman saw her throwing. He came down from the telephone pole and advised her to throw not with a windmill motion but with a slingshot motion. She followed his advice and acquired control to go with her speed, becoming a superstar pitcher with 123 no hitters and 37 perfect games!

**Letting Children Wear an Olympic Gold Medal**

In 1996, Dorothy "Dot" Richardson was a member of the United States women's softball team that won the gold medal at the Summer Olympics. Immediately after winning the gold medal, she had to fly to Los Angeles where she was completing her residency at a hospital. (Today, she is an orthopedic surgeon.) Fortunately, the hospital gave her another week off so she could do such things as meet the First Family and appear on *David Letterman*. Of course, she made up the hours of work she missed, and she gave children in the hospital a chance to wear her gold medal.

**Three Dozen Red Roses**

Ohio State University Buckeyes football coach Woody Hayes frequently performed charitable acts. One day, a woman presented Mr. Hayes with three dozen red roses at the Columbus, Ohio, airport when the team returned after a game. He asked his defensive coordinator, George Hill, to show up at the studio at 11 p.m. to prepare for the *Woody Hayes Show*, but Mr. Hayes himself didn't arrive until 11:20 p.m., explaining that he was late because he had been giving away the roses to a number of elderly patients at University Hospital. Mr. Hayes said, "There are little old ladies in that hospital, George, who are worried about whether they're going to live or die, and all we're worried about is a d*mned football game."

**A Hard Man to Figure Out**

Coach George Halas of the Chicago Bears was a hard man to figure out. Brian Piccolo bargained for months with him before getting a $500 raise, but after Mr. Piccolo got cancer and racked up thousands of dollars in hospital bills, Mr. Halas paid them.

### A Hug for a Competitor

Olga Korbut's revolutionary gymnastics feats astonished the world at the 1972 Olympic Games in Munich. Nevertheless, she was not always perfect. After receiving the low score of 7.5 on the uneven bars, she sat crying. None of her friends were around to comfort her because they were busy competing in their own events, so a member of the German Democratic Republic team, Erica Zuchold, came over and gave her a hug.

### "I Have One Final Gift for You"

After Mary Lou Retton won the all-around gold medal in women's gymnastics in the 1984 Olympic Games in Los Angeles, she became a celebrity and needed an agent. Her coach, Bela Karolyi, investigated some agents and recommended one who was acceptable to Ms. Retton and her parents. The percentages worked out this way: Ms. Retton would get 75%, the agent would get 15%, and Mr. Karolyi would get 10%. However, as soon as the contract was signed, Mr. Karolyi told Ms. Retton, "I have one final gift for you," then he signed over his 10% to her.

### A Father and a Machete

Professional golfer Chi Chi Rodriguez grew up in poverty in Puerto Rico. One day, his father noticed a boy stealing bananas from a tree in his yard, so he asked Chi Chi to bring him his machete. Chi Chi did so, thinking that something terrible was going to happen. However, his father used the machete to cut some more bananas from the tree for the boy.

### "What a Stupid I Am"

Roberto de Vicenzo had a good shot at winning the 1968 Masters Tournament in Augusta, Georgia. He and Bob Goalby finished tied with a score of 11-under-par after four days of play, and they appeared to be heading for a playoff. Unfortunately, both Mr. Vicenzo and his playing partner, Tommy Aaron, made errors. Mr. Aaron was keeping score for Mr. Vicenzo, and he mistakenly wrote "4" where "3" should have gone. Mr. Vicenzo then made the mistake of signing the scorecard instead of checking it over first. According to the rules, if a player signs an inaccurate scorecard that improves his score, that player is disqualified. But if a player signs an inaccurate scorecard that lowers his score, the player must accept that lower score. Because of the incorrect scorecard, Mr. Goalby won the Masters. Mr. Aaron felt bad because he had marked the wrong score, but Mr. Vicenzo, in a display of impressively good sportsmanship, blamed only himself. He told reporters, players, and fans in his broken English, "What a stupid I am!" A couple of years later, he won an award for good sportsmanship. He accepted the trophy, studied the inscription, and then said, "Golf writers make three mistakes spelling my name on trophy. Maybe I not the only stupid."

**Stunningly Good Sportsmanship**

Professional golfer Jack Nicklaus showed stunningly good sportsmanship at the 1969 Ryder Cup. Mr. Nicklaus was playing against Tony Jacklin, and if Mr. Nicklaus won, that meant the United States won. On the final hole, Mr. Jacklin needed to make a three-and-a-half-foot putt for Great Britain to tie the United States. Although putts of that length are not normally conceded, Mr. Nicklaus conceded it, and the two friendly nations ended up tied.

**Showing Respect to a Defeated Opponent**

When golfer Payne Stewart won the PGA Championship, beating his friend Mike Reid, he was super excited. His friend and fellow golfer Peter Jacobsen saw him in a restroom, where Mr. Stewart was so excited about winning that he was trying to run up the restroom wall. Mr. Jacobsen decided to talk to him because he worried about him showing too much inappropriate excitement in public. He told Mr. Stewart, "You just won the PGA Championship. That's huge. And I'm ecstatic for you. ... But you have to gather yourself. While you're jumping up the wall, a friend of ours is probably dying inside from having blown the tournament. When you go out there, you can't be butt-slapping and doing high fives. You have to talk about how your friend Mike Reid played great, and would have made a great PGA champion as well. You need to show some respect for him ...." Mr. Stewart took the advice and gave Mr. Reid a lot of respect and did everything the way it ought to have been done. This is a good example of one person giving wise advice and another person being wise enough to take it. And when Mr. Stewart made a great shot at Pinehurst to defeat Phil Mickelson at the U.S. Open, Mr. Stewart didn't need wise advice to do the best thing. He comforted Mr. Mickelson, whose wife was about to give birth, by telling him, "You are going to be a father. That is the greatest thing that can happen in your life. You are so lucky."

**Lots of Help from Others**

Althea Gibson received much help in her careers as a tennis and golf player. An African-American, Ms. Gibson broke racial barriers by winning Wimbledon in 1957 and 1958. Among the people who helped her was boxer Sugar Ray Robinson, who served as a positive role model and encouraged her to get an education and to pursue a career playing tennis. In addition, Dr. Hubert A. Eaton let her live with his family in Wilmington, North Carolina, while she attended high school and college and trained to be a tennis player, and Dr. Robert Walker Johnson let her live with his family in Lynchburg, Virginia, from which she traveled to play in tennis tournaments. Another boxer who helped Ms. Gibson was Joe Louis, who helped support her financially when she played in her first Wimbledon tournament in 1951—she lost in the third round. Also helping support her in that first Wimbledon competition was a group of blacks in Detroit who held a variety show and raised $770 for her. After Ms. Gibson began to break racial barriers in women's professional golf, Leonard Wirtz, director of the Ladies Professional Golf Association, supported her. Occasionally, while Ms. Gibson was allowed to play on a golf course, she was not permitted to enter its clubhouse because of her race, and so she did not have a place to eat lunch, take a shower, or change her clothes. When that happened, Mr. Wirtz pleaded her case and if that didn't work, he took stronger action. Three times, he moved a tournament from a prejudiced golf club—as shown by the club's treatment of Ms. Gibson—to a golf club that was not prejudiced and that treated Ms. Gibson well.

**"Would You Like to Learn to Play?"**

The best African-American tennis player in Richmond, Virginia, in the 1940s and 1950s was Ron Charity. One day, he noticed a little boy watching him as he practiced, and he asked the boy, "Would you like to learn to play?" The boy did want to learn how to play, so Mr. Charity taught him. Eventually, Mr. Charity was so impressed by the boy's talent that he made sure he received training at a tennis camp run by Dr. Robert Walker Johnson, a physician in Lynchburg, Virginia. When the boy, whose name was Arthur Ashe, grew up, he became the first African-American man to win the men's singles title at Wimbledon.

### U.S. Open Tickets

Tennis great Arthur Ashe once suffered a heart attack and ended up at Cornell, where his cardiologist practiced, but even then he did not forget his friends. He called up Seth Abraham and offered him his tickets for the United States Open on Super Saturday: men's semifinals and women's final—a wonderful event for tennis lovers. Mr. Abraham was astonished. Later, he said that he told him: "Arthur, you've just had a heart attack and are in the critical-care unit of the hospital, and you're worried about your blankety-blank tickets?" Mr. Ashe replied, "Yeah, I didn't want them to go to waste, and I knew that you could use them."

### A $50 Consolation Prize

John L. Sullivan used to fight all comers barefisted for a $1,000 purse; because he was such a great fighter, he was never beaten, but the person who lasted the longest in the ring with him got a consolation prize of $50. One day, a first-year Massachusetts Institute of Technology student named Alfred I. du Pont showed up to fight Mr. Sullivan—not for any glory, but because he needed the money. Mr. Sullivan was sympathetic to the student's plight and made sure to spar with Mr. du Pont long enough for him to pick up the consolation prize money. The two men became friends, and after Mr. Sullivan had retired and spent all the money he had earned from prizefighting, the now extremely wealthy Mr. du Pont gave him a monthly stipend and a small farm to live on.

### A Women's Prison

Muhammad Ali has done many good deeds, such as visiting a women's prison in California, where he kissed all the ugly women prisoners but did not kiss the pretty women prisoners. Asked why, he replied, "The good-looking ones ain't got no problem. But them ugly ones, who's gonna kiss them? If I kiss them, they got something to talk about for the rest of their lives."

### "Give Me My Room!"

Belly dancer Jodette had traveled to New York City to teach a dance workshop, but unfortunately, she discovered that the hotel had lost her reservation and given her room to someone else. Because Muhammad Ali was fighting Ken Norton, the hotels in the area were packed, and Jodette knew it would be difficult to find another room. She stood there and cried, shouting at the hotel staff, "Give me my room!" At that moment, Mr. Ali walked by with his entourage, and he ordered, "Find her a place." They found her a suite at the Hilton Hotel, and Mr. Ali paid for it. He also gave her ringside seats for his fight with Mr. Norton. A few years later, Jodette was in the Los Angeles International Airport, trying to get to Cairo, Egypt. Again, her reservation had been lost, and her seat had been given to someone else. Again, she stood at the ticket counter, crying and saying, "Give me my seat!" She felt a tap on her shoulder, turned around, and saw Mr. Ali, who asked, "*Now* what's going on?" He invited her to have lunch with him and his secretary, and by the time lunch was over, Jodette had a first-class airplane ticket to Cairo, paid for by Mr. Ali.

**Spending Money to Help People**

Muhammad Ali made a lot of money, and he spent a lot of it to help black people. One winter day, an old man wearing rags arrived at his home to ask for money: a couple of hundred dollars. Mr. Ali asked what he would do if he got the money, and the old man answered, "Go home." Mr. Ali handed over $200 and told him, "Don't stop along the way." It wasn't just black people whom Mr. Ali helped. He once heard on the news that a home for elderly Jews was going to be shut down for lack of funds, so he stopped by and wrote a check for $100,000. In addition, he helped old-time fighters who needed a job—fighters like Kid Gavilan and Ike Williams. He had no real need to put them on his payroll, but they had a real need for a job, so on his payroll they went.

**"You Tell Uncle Ellie I Was Asking About Him"**

In the early 20th century, Benny Leonard was both Jewish and the lightweight champion of the world. This made him the hero of the children of the Caplin family, one of whom would grow up to become Al Capp, creator of *Li'l Abner*. Al had an uncle named Ellie, whom he loved and who claimed to know many of the famous sports stars of his day, including Benny Leonard. Al never had a reason to doubt this claim, so when Mr. Leonard appeared at a theater in his town, Al waited by the exit so that he could meet him and tell him that he was the nephew of his friend Uncle Ellie. Things went as planned, and young Al told Mr. Leonard, "I'm Uncle Ellie's nephew, Benny." Mr. Leonard paused, recognized that this boy's uncle had tried to make himself a hero in the boy's eyes by pretending to be his friend, and said, "How is Uncle Ellie? You tell Uncle Ellie I was asking about him. Send him my best. OK, kid?" Uncle Ellie was understandably nervous later when Al said that he had met Benny Leonard, and he was understandably relieved when Al said that Mr. Leonard had sent him his best.

### Helping a Dance Troupe

Heavyweight fighter Joe Louis was very generous with his money. Whenever dancer Norma Miller needed money, she knew that she could talk to him and get help. One day, she and her dance troupe were broke. They had a dance date coming up, and they needed to get their costumes out of the cleaners, but Ms. Miller had no money to pay the cleaners' bill. She called Mr. Louis, and he came right over with some of his friends. Mr. Louis was wearing a loud tie, which his friends made fun of, so Mr. Louis took off the tie and dropped it in Ms. Miller's lap, leaning over for a moment to whisper, "The money's in the tie."

### "It's Coming Back to You"

Julie Snellings was a wonderful female jockey in 1977. In that year she wrote a letter to an old boyfriend named Jackie Fires, who was also a jockey and who had been paralyzed when he took a spill off a horse at River Downs. The letter was hard to write, and she began it by writing, "You're the toughest guy I ever met." As preparation for writing the letter, she tried to feel as if she had to get out of bed although her legs were paralyzed. She also wrote Mr. Fires, "If anyone can do it, you can." A month later, she took a spill off a horse and was paralyzed. Soon after, she received a telephone call from Mr. Fires, who told her, "Remember the letter you wrote to me? I put a return address on it, and it's coming back to you."

### Sharing the Wealth

Don Haskins coached his Texas Western University basketball team to an upset NCAA Championship victory against powerhouse Kentucky in 1966. Forty years later, the movie *Glory Road* appeared, based on the events of that wonderful season. Mr. Haskins was supposed to receive approximately $375,000, while each of the players was supposed to receive approximately $7,500 each, but when Mr. Haskins discovered how little the players were receiving, he insisted that everyone receive equal shares. Everyone, including Mr. Haskins, received approximately $37,000.

### Dropping Out of School

While Charles Barkley was playing professional basketball for the Philadelphia 76ers, the team received a telephone call from a Florida high school basketball coach. The coach had recently cut a player from the team, and now the boy was thinking of dropping out of school. Since Mr. Barkley was the boy's hero, the coach asked whether he would be willing to speak with the boy and convince him to stay in school. Mr. Barkley was willing, and he called the boy's home from the Sixers' front office. Unfortunately, the boy wasn't home then, so Mr. Barkley called the boy later that night from his own home. This time, he reached the boy, and after talking to him for an hour, he convinced him to stay in school.

**Autographs for a Fan**

As the United States women's national basketball team—which later won gold at the 1996 Olympic Games—was leaving the Civic Center in Providence, Rhode Island, the team members saw a girl holding an autograph book running after their bus. The girl started crying, the women's team members made the driver stop the bus, and every player got out and signed the girl's autograph book. Star player Sheryl Swopes said later, "It didn't take but two minutes to turn the saddest girl in Rhode Island into the happiest."

**"Can I *Please* Borrow Your Tights?"**

Good deeds take various forms, ranging from saving someone from dying to saving someone from embarrassment. At the 2002 Winter Olympic Games, figure skater Sasha Cohen went through security checkpoint after security checkpoint, and at each checkpoint, her bag containing her skating dress and tights was emptied, examined, and then refilled. Unfortunately, when it was time for Sasha to get dressed for the competition shortly before going on the ice, she discovered that her tights were missing. Somehow, they had been left behind at a security checkpoint. Not enough time remained for her mother to go to their hotel to get a pair of tights, so Sasha thought that she would not be able to compete at the Olympics—no tights, no competition. Fortunately, another figure skater, Fumie Suguri, walked into the dressing room. She had finished competing and was ready to get into her street clothing. Sasha said, "Fumie! Can I *please* borrow your tights?" Fumie said, "Sure," and stripped them off. Sasha had only a few minutes left to get ready, and she was shaking at the thought of almost not being able to compete. (In 2002, she finished fourth, and four years later, she won the silver medal.)

**Breakfast in Bed**

Russian ice skater Sergei Mikhailovich Grinkov once made his wife and pairs skating partner, Ekaterina Gordeeva, breakfast in bed for her birthday, because that is one of the presents she dearly wanted. He woke up before his wife, and slipped out of bed, but making breakfast did not come easily to him—he had to make the coffee twice, because the first time he somehow messed up. He also decided to get flowers to brighten the breakfast tray, but he was afraid that he would awaken his wife when he started the car, so he pushed the car out of the garage and away from the house before starting it. This breakfast was one of the best surprises he ever gave his wife.

**Oklahoma City**

A month after the 1995 Oklahoma City bombing, an ice skating tour performed at Oklahoma City. Of course, everyone was aware of the tragedy, and skater Brian Boitano suggested that the skaters all donate their fees toward the building of a new day care center to replace the one destroyed in the bombing. Everyone thought it was a great idea, and they contributed $125,000 toward the new day care center.

**"This is Not for Skating"**

Just before Dorothy Hamill left to compete in her second World Championship, Peggy Fleming's mother, Doris, gave her $100, saying, "This is not for skating. This is for you, Dorothy. Buy yourself something pretty with it." In addition, Mrs. Fleming had helped take care of Dorothy when Dorothy was ill. Ms. Hamill writes that Mrs. Fleming "seemed to know just what to do at any given moment, and her gift meant a lot to me."

**Music to Ice Dance By**

When they were very young ice dancers, Jayne Torvill and Christopher Dean ran into a problem. They needed music to skate to, which meant they needed to listen to a lot of music, yet they had very little money to buy record albums. In addition, they sometimes bought an album because they liked the cover art and then were disappointed with the music when they listened to it. Fortunately, they did an interview with BBC Radio Nottingham, and they noticed that it had a huge music library filled with thousands of albums. They asked for permission to use the music library, which was very kindly granted to them with the result that they were able to find music to dance to without spending more money than they could afford. Torvill and Dean won the

Olympic gold medal in 1984, skating to Ravel's "Bolero" and earning perfect 6.0's for artistic impression from *all* the judges.

**Memorializing a Good Deed**

The Iditarod in Alaska is a 1,049-mile dog sled race that memorializes a 1925 outbreak of diphtheria in Nome, Alaska. The diphtheria vaccine was carried part way to Nome by railroad, but it took dog sleds to carry the vaccine the rest of the way. Twenty volunteers loaded up their dog sleds and reached Nome in five days and seven hours, saving the town.

**"Your Brakes are on Fire! Try and Stop Your Truck!"**

In 1974, Jeana Day Felts had trouble driving her truck on a mountain. Driving up the mountain, everything was fine, but Ms. Felts didn't know that when you drive a truck down a mountain, you need to be in a low gear to avoid burning up your brakes. She was having trouble, and a man drove next to her and shouted, "Your brakes are on fire! Try and stop your truck!" With her brakes smoking, she was headed into a curve too fast. Fortunately, the man drove in front of her and let her ease the truck into his car, slowing it down until it stopped. After the brakes had cooled down, he drove the truck down the mountain for her, after pointing out, "If you'd gone an extra curve or two, you'd have ended your life in a ravine." A cowgirl, Ms. Felts earned the title of World Champion Barrel Racer later that year.

# Chapter 3: AUTHORS

**Helping the Oppressed**

Robert Benchley was on the side of the oppressed. After a desk clerk at a Hollywood hotel refused to allow him to host an African-American bandleader in his room, Mr. Benchley immediately checked out of the hotel. During the Depression, some people felt that theater critics were taking food away from the mouths of actors by writing bad reviews that resulted in the closing of plays, but even before the criticism was made, Mr. Benchley had donated some of the royalties from his books to Actors Equity. While he was working at *Life*, an executive wanted his employees to donate 10 percent of their salaries to the construction fund of the Cathedral of St. John the Divine, but Mr. Benchley felt that this was extorting money from secretaries who needed their jobs and at the risk of losing his own job he advised them to do no such thing.

**A Drunken Prostitute**

The writer Samuel Johnson once found a drunken prostitute lying in Fleet Street in London, England. He asked her where she lived, and then he carried her on his back to the address she named.

**Children Sleeping in the Street**

Samuel Johnson performed many acts of charity in addition to giving much of his pension money to charity. Sometimes, he saw children wearing rags sleeping in the streets and he slipped money into their palms so when they awoke the next morning, they could buy breakfast.

**A Well-Loved Book**

Johanna Hurwitz, author of *Busybody Nora*, worked as a school librarian. While going through the shelves looking for books too old and battered to be read any more, she came across a worn-out copy of a novel by one of her favorite authors for children: Carolyn Haywood. Because she wanted Ms. Haywood to see how loved her book was—it had been read to pieces—she wrapped it and sent it as a gift to her.

**A Kind Recluse**

In later life, poet Emily Dickinson was practically a recluse in her home in Amherst, Massachusetts; however, she sometimes lowered from an upstairs window a basket of sweets to children playing near her home.

## Charitable Ghostwriters

When humorous poet Don Marquis, author of *archy and mehitabel*, was very ill following a stroke, a group of his friends got together, wrote a short story titled "Tablecloth," and sold it both to the *Saturday Evening Post* and to the movie industry to raise money for his care. The name that appeared on the short story was "Don Marquis," but the real authors were Gene Fowler, Nunnally Johnson, Grover Jones, and Patterson McNutt.

## Forgiving a Killer

Mary Carter Smith taught for many years in inner-city Baltimore (Maryland) schools, she co-founded a Big Sister-Little Sister program in Baltimore, and she became a famous African-American *griot* (storyteller). Nevertheless, her life contained a share of tragedy. Her only son, Ricardo Rogers Carter, was murdered at 29 years of age in Baltimore on 6 January 1978. Ms. Smith attended the trial, where she noticed that the woman who had stabbed her son to death did not seem remorseful. A year after the woman had been sentenced to prison, Ms. Carter gave a storytelling performance at the prison in which the woman was serving her sentence. After the performance, Ms. Carter met and talked with the woman, who asked Ms. Carter to forgive her and who now seemed to be a troubled person looking for help. Ms. Carter did forgive the woman, and she did help her. To secure an early release from prison, the woman needed a job, and Ms. Carter helped her find one.

## Mixed Marriage

While living in Jackson, Mississippi, in the 1960s, Mel Leventhal and Alice Walker faced prejudice because of their mixed marriage—he was white, and she was black. For protection, they relied on their neighbors, who telephoned them when they saw strange white people driving around in the neighborhood. If the strange white people were very close, their neighbors would stand out on their porch to let the strangers know that there would be witnesses to any violence that might occur.

## "Why Don't You Go Somewhere and Get Warm?"

As a boy, comic author H. Allen Smith sold newspapers. On a bitterly cold day, he was out hawking his papers when a man walked up to him and asked him, "Why don't you go somewhere and get warm?" Young H. Allen said, "I have to sell the rest of my papers first." The man bought all the rest of the newspapers and told him, "Go on home and get warm."

**Stopping Sexual Harassment**

Comic writer Robert Benchley knew how to stop sexual harassment. At a gathering in his Hollywood bungalow, a drunken writer was trying to get over-friendly with the wife of an absent bandleader. Just as the writer put his hand on the woman's knee, Mr. Benchley walked up and asked the wife quietly, "I'm sorry. Is my friend becoming offensive?" The drunken writer quickly left.

**Don't Pray for Me**

Dame Muriel Spark wrote such famous novels as *The Prime of Miss Jean Brodie*, but she occasionally suffered from poverty. During one lean period, she was supported financially by fellow novelist Graham Greene, but he made two conditions for his support: 1) She must never thank him, and 2) She must never pray for him.

**"You Haven't Been Mean to Me in Three Days!"**

For a while, *MAD* magazine writer Dick DeBartolo owned a houseboat, but it sank. Fortunately, his insurance covered the houseboat. Unfortunately, his insurance did not cover the possessions on the houseboat. His boss, publisher William M. Gaines, asked him if he regretted losing one possession in particular, and he answered that he regretted losing a 35mm camera. Mr. Gaines immediately told him to buy another camera—and to send the bill to him. Mr. DeBartolo was so overcome by Mr. Gaines's kindness that he didn't insult him for a few days—which was actually a no-no in those days at *MAD*. Ordinarily, Mr. DeBartolo would have been doing such things as opening Mr. Gaines' door so that visitors could see him, and then announcing, "That blithering idiot is William M. Gaines!" or "It's cold in here because Mr. Gaines died two years ago, but we like to leave him propped up at his desk for this tour!" (After Mr. DeBartolo stopped insulting Mr. Gaines, the great publisher buzzed his office to complain, "Are you mad at me? You haven't been mean to me in three days!" Mr. DeBartolo replied by screaming into the receiver, "I WAS MEAN TO YOU JUST THIS MORNING, BUT YOU'RE SO OLD AND SENILE, YOU DON'T REMEMBER!" This cheered Mr. Gaines up.

**Good Deeds for Small Children**

Stan and Jan Berenstain, creators of the Berenstain Bears, have used their celebrity to do many good deeds. As a child, Stan suffered from amblyopia or lazy eye; unfortunately, his condition was not diagnosed early enough for him to cure it by wearing an eye patch over his strong eye, which would have forced his lazy eye to work harder. Therefore, when a grandmother e-mailed Stan about her five-year-old granddaughter who had been diagnosed with amblyopia and who was embarrassed about wearing the eye patch, Stan immediately e-mailed the granddaughter and encouraged her to wear the eye patch. Later, they heard back from the grandmother—the five-year-old girl was wearing it. On another occasion, they heard about a little girl with terminal cancer in New York City's Sloan-Kettering cancer hospital. The little girl wanted a Sister Bear doll. They sent her one, and later they learned that she had died with it in her arms.

**Fallen Nestlings**

When Chris Crutcher, author of the young adult novel *Stotan!*, was very young, he watched the nest that a bird had built on top of a pillar that was part of his family's porch, and he was very happy when the eggs hatched and the nestlings started peeping. One day, however, he was startled to hear peeping coming not from the nest on top of the pillar but from inside the pillar itself. Somehow, the nestlings had fallen through a hole on top of the pillar and were now inside the pillar itself. Panicked, he ran to his grandfather for help. Fortunately, his grandfather took care of the problem, using a hand jigsaw to cut out a hole at the bottom of the pillar, where the nestlings were. The mother bird found the nestlings and started feeding them, and after the nestlings had grown up and flew away, Chris' grandfather repaired both the hole at the top of the pillar and the hole he had cut out at the bottom of the pillar.

**Completely Unable to Speak**

As a very young financial writer—and the only woman financial writer—for the *New York Post*, Sylvia Porter went to a huge bankers' convention, where she took many notes. Then she and the male reporters ran for the telephones so they could call in their articles to a rewrite man. However, when Ms. Porter was transferred to the rewrite man, she froze and was completely unable to speak—a common occurrence for young reporters. Fortunately, a male reporter for a rival publication saw what was happening, so he took her phone and called in her story for her. Ms. Porter says, "He was just wonderful. At that moment, I couldn't have talked if my life depended on it." Afterward, of course, Ms. Porter became an internationally famous financial writer.

**"Take This Book of Poems and Memorize One for Me"**

When African-American author Maya Angelou was a child, she was raped, and as a result she stopped talking, except to her brother. The person who convinced her to begin talking to other people again was an African-American woman named Mrs. Bertha Flowers who gave the nine-year-old girl treats and read out loud to her Charles Dickens' *Tale of Two Cities*. She also gave her a book and requested, "Take this book of poems and memorize one for me. Next time you pay me a visit, I want you to recite." Young Maya did. She said later about Mrs. Flowers, "It was through her and poetry that I began to talk."

**"Well, Man, It Was Your Words"**

The late comedian Dick Gregory was a deeply moral man. His autobiography titled *Nigger* was co-authored by Richard Lipsyte. When a movie company took out on an option on the book, Mr. Gregory tore up his old contract just so Mr. Lipsyte could get some money from the movie option. He told Mr. Lipsyte, "Well, man, it was your words."

# Chapter 4: ART

**Putting Talent to the Test**

Early in his career, Winslow Homer wondered if he had enough talent to make it as an artist, and he decided to put his talent to a test. He sent two paintings to an art dealer. If the two paintings, which were good, sold for the prices he had set for them, he would paint serious works of art. If not, he would continue to work as an illustrator for magazines. Winslow confided his plan to Charles, his brother, and Charles secretly went to the art dealer and bought the two paintings for the prices that Winslow had set for them. Years later, Winslow discovered what Charles had done, and by then Winslow had earned a reputation as a major artist.

**Helping a Migrant Mother**

In 1935, Dorothea Lange took a photograph that resulted in a great deal of good. Migrant workers came to Nipomo, California, to pick the peas at a farm; unfortunately, bad weather ruined the crop, leaving the migrant workers, who were destitute, with no way to earn money to buy food. Ms. Lange visited the migrant workers, and she saw a married woman with seven children huddled in a tent. The woman had sold the tires off her car to get money to buy food. Ms. Lange's photograph of the woman and her children appeared in two San Francisco newspapers, and Americans came together to help the migrant workers, sending 22,000 pounds of food to the camp of the migrant workers. The migrant mother lived for close to another 50 years.

**Turnips and Bruised Fruit**

During the Great Depression, people sometimes found it difficult to live on what they made, even when they had a job. Ed Smith started work at the Walt Disney studio, where he made a beginning salary that led to his living on turnips and bruised fruit. One day at work, because of malnutrition, he passed out. Later, his boss, Ben Sharpsteen, talked to *his* boss, Walt Disney himself, and recommended that the wages of beginning workers be raised. Mr. Disney agreed, and he raised the beginning salaries high enough that people such as Mr. Smith could afford to eat at a nearby greasy spoon restaurant with the other Disney employees.

**Sensitivity Despite Being Provoked**

Some people are capable of great sensitivity even when they themselves are treated badly. A Jewish grocer once treated badly a couple of Mexican-Americans: Judy Baca and her grandmother. Judy was a child at the time, and she later grew up to become a community artist and educator—she painted *The Great Wall of Los Angeles*, which beautified a San Fernando Valley flood control channel. Judy was understandably upset, but her grandmother noticed that a number was tattooed on the wrist of the Jewish grocer. Her grandmother told young Judy that the Jewish grocer had suffered terribly, and she taught her about the concentration camps and the Holocaust.

**A Wealthy White Woman**

Early in his career, African-American artist Palmer Hayden made money by cleaning other people's homes. However, when Alice Dyke, a wealthy white woman for whom he worked, discovered that he painted, she viewed some of his canvases and recommended that he enter them in the Harmon Foundation art competition for 1926. He won the gold medal and $400 in the competition, and with a generous $4,000 gift from Ms. Dyke, he set sail for Paris and painted there for six years.

**Good Salaries During the Depression**

Eleanor Brown was an early interior decorator, having founded her decorating firm, McMillen, Inc., in 1924. During the Great Depression, McMillen, Inc., performed a remarkable good deed. Although little or no business was to be found, McMillen, Inc., paid good salaries to its ten employees to build models of houses. They were one and a half inches to the foot, and they contained miniature furniture, carpets, crystal chandeliers, lamps and wall brackets, china, and bathroom fixtures. After they had been created, they were exhibited around the country. How could the firm afford to pay good salaries to ten employees to make these model houses? Actually, it couldn't. It lost money all throughout the Depression; fortunately, the Depression ended and business picked up again.

# Chapter 5: MUSIC

**Bad Wine and Good Manners**

While conducting at the Salzburg Festival, Arturo Toscanini took pains to preserve his privacy. One day, he went to an obscure restaurant where he hoped not to be noticed, but he was recognized instantly. The proprietor of the restaurant gave the Maestro the best seat and then brought him the best wine available at the restaurant. A friend tasted the wine, discovered that it was awful, and advised Mr. Toscanini (in a foreign language the proprietor didn't understand) not to drink it. However, Mr. Toscanini drank the wine anyway, and complimented the proprietor on it. Later, Mr. Toscanini explained, "He [the proprietor] was so kind. I could not refuse."

**Honoring World War I Soldiers**

Opera singer Mary Garden performed an impressive good deed for a village named Peille on a mountain of Monte Carlo that wished to honor its soldiers who had died in World War I. After seeing a circular asking for funds to build a statue, she saw the village's Mayor and said she wanted to help. During her concerts in America that season, she set the money she earned aside and after the concert season was over, she took the money and gave it to the Mayor. The statue the villagers built showed a soldier at the point of dying after being hit with a bullet in the chest. After the statue had been built, enough money was left over to build a public square for such activities as festivals and dances. Later, Ms. Garden read a letter in the *New York Herald* (Paris edition) from a man who wondered "why Mary Garden had put all that money and love into that little village." Ms. Garden writes, "I didn't bother to answer the letter, because any man asking that kind of question would never understand the feeling I had put into the statue."

**Kindness in Prison**

Opera singer Caterina Gabrielli once declined to perform for the viceroy of Sicily, and as a result she was sentenced to 12 days in prison. She used her time in prison well, singing free concerts for the other inmates, and she gave them money and paid off many of their debts. When she got out of prison, the people whom she had freed from prison by paying their debts met her with applause.

**Honoring a Widow**

Enrico Caruso was discovered by baritone Edouard Missiano, who took him to his own voice teacher for lessons so his voice could be properly trained. Years later, Mr. Caruso was a great star, while Mr. Missiano's fortunes had declined. Mr. Caruso paid his debt by getting Mr. Missiano work at the Met, where he appeared in minor roles in several operas. When Mr. Missiano died before appearing in *La Gioconda*, Mr. Caruso sent the body to his benefactor's widow and three children at his own expense. He also sent a large check—his own fee for starring in *La Gioconda*.

**A Generous Autograph Signer**

Enrico Caruso could be very generous. One day he needed a pen to sign autographs, so an electrician lent him a $5 pen he was very proud of—$5 was a lot of money back then. Unfortunately, after signing some autographs Mr. Caruso absent-mindedly put the pen in his pocket and walked off with it. Because Mr. Caruso was a VIP, the electrician didn't say anything, and he thought that he had seen the last of his pen. But the very next day, the electrician received a package from Mr. Caruso. Inside the package was his $5 pen, and wrapped around the pen was a $20 bill.

**Going Through the Papers of a Deceased Husband**

After Enrico Caruso died, his wife, Dorothy, went through his papers. One item she found was a list of all the people her husband had supported financially during his life. In addition to the names of scores of relatives, the list contained the names of 120 men and women, each of whom had performed a kindness for Mr. Caruso that he had never forgotten and each of whom he rewarded with money after he became rich and famous.

**A Rescue from the Nazis**

French soprano Germaine Lubin was thought to sympathize with the Nazis during World War II, but she did some very impressive good deeds. Marya Freund, the mother of bass Doda Conrad, was in an old folks home. Ms. Lubin sent her a message that a car would come for her at a certain time; she should get in the car, which would take her to safety. The rescue came off as planned, and when the Nazis arrived to arrest Ms. Freund, she was gone.

**An Impromptu Concert**

Soprano Kirsten Flagstad could be a very generous person. While journeying to Australia, she became friends with Father James Carroll. In Melbourne, she met Father Carroll again and learned that he was visiting his brother, a priest, whom he had not seen for 17 years, and his sister, a nun, whom he had not seen for 37 years. Ms. Flagstad invited Father Carroll, his brother and sister, and an additional nun to visit her at her hotel the next day. Because Ms. Flagstad realized that the nuns did not go to public concerts, she sang several songs for them.

### "Have Courage"

The first time Frances Alda sang at the Metropolitan Opera, she received bad reviews, which disheartened her. However, after reading the bad reviews, she received a huge basket of roses and a note from the celebrated opera singer Madame Lillian Nordica, whom she had never met. The note said, "There was never a young singer who appeared at the Metropolitan who wasn't severely criticized on her début. Melba, Sembrich, Farrar [all famous opera singers], myself ... all of us have gone through what you are going through today. Have courage." Ms. Alda never forgot the kindness of Ms. Nordica. Ms. Alda continued to sing at the Metropolitan, and eventually she conquered the New York critics.

### A Proud Man

Gustav Charpentier, the creator both of the words and music of the opera *Louise*, was a proud man, even while he was impoverished before the success of *Louise*. André Messager once saw him in his rooms as he was lying in bed with nothing but an overcoat for cover. Still, Mr. Charpentier was insulted when Mr. Messager offered to help him. While *Louise* was in rehearsal, the company tried to figure out a way to help Mr. Charpentier without his knowing what they were doing. Finally, they decided to offer free milk and sandwiches during rehearsal rest breaks. Because everyone ate the food, Mr. Charpentier didn't know that it had been brought in because of him. The success of his opera was very gratifying to Mr. Charpentier. Years later, he told Mr. Messager, "The success of *Louise* gave my mother a beefsteak every day for years."

### "Would You Deprive Your Mother?"

Long-distance telephone rates used to be much higher than they are now. One day, opera/lieder singer Kathleen Ferrier met Ena Mitchell's son and learned that he had been offered a permanent post in a prestigious orchestra. Ms. Ferrier told him, "You must telephone and tell your mother." He replied, "Yes, I shall do that this evening, when the long-distance charges are reduced."

Instead, Ms. Ferrier insisted that he use her telephone, saying, "Would you deprive your mother of six hours of happiness?"

**A World-Famous Opera Singer (and Wet Nurse)**

Early in her career as an opera singer, Ernestine Schumann-Heink had both an infant and a great need to make money to support her family. Therefore, she weaned her infant and put it on the bottle so that she could go to Leipzig and sing for money. However, she soon discovered that she had made a miscalculation. Her breasts were full of milk, which made her very uncomfortable. Fortunately, an impoverished woman in the chorus heard of her plight and asked Ms. Schumann-Heink to nurse her own two-month-old infant. The chorus singer was too ill and weak to nurse the infant, and she was too impoverished to buy milk for it. Ms. Schumann-Heink looked at the infant and saw that it was dying of starvation. Therefore, she nursed the infant every two hours while she was singing in Leipzig, and by the time she left the city, the infant was much, much stronger than she had found it. Sixteen years later, Ms. Schumann-Heink returned to Leipzig, and the woman who had been in the chorus visited her—along with the very healthy 16-year-old girl whom Ms. Schumann-Heink had nursed.

Odd as it may sound, this is not the only starving infant whom Ms. Schumann-Heink nursed. In Hamburg, she knew of an impoverished mother who was unable to nurse her infant, so Ms. Schumann-Heink nursed it for her. Years afterward, the mother visited her in the company of her 6-foot-tall son and then announced that he was the infant whom Ms. Schumann-Heink had nursed. (The young man was embarrassed—he turned red and then ran out of the room.)

**Flowers at a Farewell Performance**

On 15 February 1900, opera singer Leo Slezak married Fräulein Wertheim. Although the day was mostly dark and dreary, at the end of the wedding, when the priest said, "I now pronounce you man and wife," a ray of sunlight broke through the clouds and shone on the kneeling couple. They stayed together until death parted them. Fräulein Wertheim had been in show business, but she retired after agreeing to be married. Mr. Slezak wanted lots of flowers present at her farewell performance, so he went from flower shop to flower shop, buying 25 baskets and bouquets to be sent to her, and disguising his handwriting so that she would think the flowers were sent to her from fans.

### Generosity at a Restaurant

Opera singer Helen Traubel once lunched in New York at a small French restaurant. At the table next to hers, a soldier and his new wife were having a wedding party. Ms. Traubel was sitting near enough to overhear the bride tell a friend, "This is a nice wedding, but I've always wanted the kind where someone sings, 'Oh, Promise Me.'" Ms. Traubel offered her services—gratis—and the bride cried with happiness when Ms. Traubel sang the song.

### Free Food

When World War I suddenly broke out, small change seemed to disappear from France, and so Russian bass Feodor Chaliapine could not get change when he paid for a meal with banknotes of 50 or 100 francs—which was all he had after being stranded in the French countryside because of the war. Therefore, to get his money's worth, he used to become acquainted with poor, hungry people he met in the street and invite them to eat with him.

### Generosity During Auditions

Sir Rudolf Bing listened to thousands of auditions, and of course, the vast majority of these auditions did not result in job offers. However, Sir Rudolf always performed a good deed at these auditions, even when he knew after the first note had been sung that the singer was not right for the Met. Therefore, he always allowed the singer to sing two numbers. According to Sir Bing, "It's just too humiliating to terminate an audition after the first number."

### The Great Man Writes

In 1905, a musician named Vincent d'Indy conducted a concert in Strasbourg. His guide on his walks around the city was Charles Munch, who later became a renowned conductor himself. Mr. Munch felt privileged to be allowed to carry Mr. d'Indy's scores to the concert hall. He felt even more privileged to receive, after Mr. d'Indy had gone back to Paris, a thank-you note written by the great man himself. At the time, Mr. Munch was only 14 years old.

### "We Will Now Talk to Each Other in Tones"

Ludwig van Beethoven comforted Baroness von Ertmann after the death of one of her children by saying to her, "We will now talk to each other in tones," then playing the piano for over an hour for her. The Baroness said later, "He told me everything with his music, and at last brought me comfort."

### Generosity as a Friend Lay Dying

As a friend of the 19th-century pianist Richard Hoffman lay dying, he stopped by her home and played several selections on her piano outside her bedroom. After he finished her favorite piece, Schubert's "Wanderer," the nurse appeared to let him know that his friend had died. Mr. Hoffman's wife hoped that the friend had heard the strains of her favorite music as she journeyed to a new life.

### Giving More Than Required

When he was a Harvard student, world-renowned cellist Yo-Yo Ma played often at concerts in and around Boston. He became very popular, and one day when one of his concerts was sold out, he gave a free concert for those who were unable to obtain tickets—he sat in the theater lobby and played Bach cello suites. Later in his career, when he was an international success, he still would often give more than required. For example, many guest cello soloists play in the first half of a concert, and then they are finished for the night. However, Mr. Ma would sometimes play as part of the orchestra in the second half of the concert—doing this with the Philadelphia Orchestra was especially enjoyable for him. He says, "It is an honor to play the back stands of the Philadelphia Orchestra. It's incredible the way those players listen, the knowledge they have. I admire it so much. And I feel the thrill of being part of something that's greater than the sum of its parts—being accepted as part of the team."

### Generosity in the Service of Music

Sir Thomas Beecham could be very generous in the service of music. In 1929, an announcement appeared in the London *Times* announcing the demise of the Oxford Subscription Concerts due to financial difficulties. Sir Thomas immediately telephoned to offer his services as a conductor free. Since he was a celebrity conductor, his concerts were well attended and profitable enough to save the concert series. In addition, in 1931, he telephoned music critic Frank Howes to offer help after learning that Mr. Howes was writing the program notes for the Leeds Festival, of which Sir Thomas was the principal conductor. Mr. Howes remarked that he needed the score of the *Mass of Life*, and Sir Thomas immediately lent it to him.

### A Private Concert

Opera singer Richard Crooks regularly exchanged letters with an 18-year-old woman fan in California, and when he was scheduled to sing near her home, he sent her a pair of tickets. Unfortunately, on the day of the concert he received a telephone call from the mother of her correspondent. The 18-year-old fan was an invalid who received much pleasure from listening to Mr. Crooks on the radio, but she was unable to attend the concert. Being a very kind man, Mr. Crooks sent a grand piano out to the young woman's home, and he sang to her in person all the songs he was scheduled to sing later that night.

## A Concert Over the Telephone

Tenor and movie star Mario Lanza was capable of great kindness. Josephine Fasano once called Mr. Lanza's house while he was out and asked if the tenor would speak to Raphaela, her 10-year-old daughter, who was a great fan and who was dying of leukemia. The man who answered the telephone said that he would give Mr. Lanza the message. Of course, Ms. Fasano hung up the telephone, thinking that nothing would happen, but Mr. Lanza called the following afternoon and gave Raphaela a 10-minute concert over the telephone. For Raphaela's 11th birthday, he flew Raphaela, her mother, and a private nurse to his home, where she spent five days. He also gave her a party at his movie studio. After Raphaela died, she was buried with one of Mr. Lanza's gifts around her neck: a sterling silver religious medal.

## Something to Cheer You Up

Johannes Brahms was a successful composer who made a good living from his music, but his father was proud and refused to accept financial support from him. One day, Mr. Brahms told his father, "Music is a great comfort. If you ever feel discouraged, look at the score of Handel's *Saul* that I have placed in your library, and it will cheer you up." One day, Mr. Brahms' father needed cheering up, so he looked at the score of Handel's *Saul*. He discovered that in between each page of the score, his son had placed money.

## Homeless in Chicago

When Oprah Winfrey was 14 years old, she wandered the streets of Chicago, homeless, and she needed help. Aretha Franklin, on the other hand, was a highly successful singer. One day, a limousine pulled up to a hotel and Ms. Franklin got out. Young Oprah saw her, ran up to her, and began pouring out her story. Before they reached the door of the hotel, Ms. Franklin had placed $100 into Oprah's hands.

## Generosity with Music Lessons

African-American singer/pianist Nina Simone, née Eunice Waymon, exhibited much music talent at an early age. Her mother worked as a housekeeper for a white family, the Millers. Mrs. Miller heard that young Eunice had musical talent, so she visited the Waymons' church so she could hear young Eunice perform. Impressed by what she had heard, she knew that Eunice would benefit from studying music. Since the Waymons could not afford to pay for the lessons, Mrs. Miller offered to pay for one year's worth of lessons. At the end of that time, Eunice's music teacher, an Englishwoman named Muriel Massinovitch, started the Eunice Waymon Fund. She got publicity for Eunice, and many people and churches contributed money for her music lessons. The money lasted throughout her teenage years and even paid for extra lessons while Eunice studied at New York City's Julliard School of Music.

**Generosity on a Ship**

In 1959, Duke Ellington decided to take his band on a European tour. Some band members flew across the ocean, but Duke and seven members of the band decided to sail across. Of course, he was treated with respect and ate frequently at the captain's table, and some of the first-class passengers asked him for a concert. On the last night of the voyage, Duke and the seven band members with him played for the captain and the first-class passengers, but Duke and his band members didn't stop there. They played next for the passengers sailing in cabin class, then they played for the passengers sailing in tourist class, and finally they played for the crewmen in the crew's quarters. According to Michael, Duke's nephew, "That's how he was about not leaving anybody out. He used to say, 'I never put anybody in a secondary position.'"

**A Ton of Coal**

During the Great Depression, jazz musician Louis Armstrong performed in an impoverished section of Baltimore, Maryland. Knowing that times were tough and that people were suffering from the very cold weather because they couldn't afford to buy coal, Mr. Armstrong bought a ton of coal, had it delivered to where the impoverished people lived, and invited them to help themselves to it.

**A "Wicked" Sense of Humor?**

Jazz violinist Joe Venuti had a wicked sense of humor. At a time of high unemployment, he telephoned 37 bass fiddle players and told them all that he had a job for them and to meet him at 8 p.m. Saturday at the corner of 52th Street and Broadway. All the bass fiddlers arrived, carrying their musical instruments and clogging up pedestrian traffic. Mr. Venuti circled the block several times in a car, laughing at all the confusion he had created. Maybe his sense of humor wasn't so wicked, after all—he paid every one of the bass fiddlers a night's wages.

### Selling Coats at a Profit

Al Jolson made a fortune in show business and had loads of money, but his father worried that Al was being extravagant whenever Al bought him an expensive present. Therefore, Al always told his father that the present cost much less than it really had. Once Al paid $140 for a camel's hair coat for his father, but he told his father that he had paid $35 each for three of them. Soon afterward, his father wrote to tell him that he had sold the $35 coat for $40 and to send him the other two coats, as he could sell those at a profit, too.

### Generosity with a Loan

Faron Young recorded Willie Nelson's "Hello Walls" and had a huge hit. Because Mr. Nelson needed money, he offered to sell the song to Mr. Young for $500. Mr. Young declined to buy the song, saying to Mr. Nelson, "You're crazy! That song has already sold more than that. Here's the five hundred. Pay me back when you have it." Later, Mr. Nelson received his first royalty check for the song—the check was for $20,000. Mr. Nelson immediately went in search of Mr. Young, and when he found him, he gave him a big kiss right on the mouth.

### A Good Deed in a Sad Life

Nancy Spungen lived a sad life with sad sex and bad drugs in some of the sub-cultures of New York and London, and her life ended with a stab wound in her abdomen, but she performed a remarkable good deed in her short life. While in London, Arturo Vega, the lighting director and graphic designer for the punk-rock group Ramones, was wearing a black leather jacket, which was the part of the uniform of the group. Unfortunately, it was also part of the uniform that punks wore in the days when London mods and punks beat each other up. Several mods came toward Arturo and Nancy as they were walking around, and Arturo, who did not know the danger he was in, was looking forward to meeting the mods. Fortunately, Nancy knew that he was in danger, so she pushed him in a doorway and stood in front of him. The mods tried to get at Arturo, who asked, "Why do they wanna kill me?" Nancy kept standing in front of Arturo, protecting him. Arturo says that the mods tried to "beat me up. They tried to hit me, but Nancy stood there. She stood in front of me and she saved me. Yeah, Nancy saved me."

# Chapter 6: DANCE

**The Perfect Gifts for a Ballerina**

Cyril Beaumont, a scholar of the ballet and collector of ballet memorabilia, knew how to give good gifts—and he knew how much his friend Alicia Markova respected the great ballerina Marie Taglioni. On the night that Ms. Markova danced the full-length *Swan Lake* at Sadler's Wells for the first time, Mr. Beaumont gave her a letter written by Ms. Taglioni. And in 1948, when Ms. Markova was going to dance the lead in the first-ever performance of *Giselle* in England, he sent her a package marked "Urgent. To be Opened on Receipt." Inside was a reel of mending silk and a note from Mr. Beaumont: "This reel is from Taglioni's workbox. Break off a piece and wear it in your shoe for luck tonight."

**The Very Kind Mr. B**

While on her first tour to Europe, a young dancer, Suzanne Farrell, mentioned to choreographer George Balanchine—known to his friends as Mr. B—that her hotel room was a little "rougher" than she had expected. He said, "I think there is an extra room at my hotel. Maybe you could move in there." She did move in, and she was delighted with the very large room—until she noticed that Mr. Balanchine's room was the size of a closet. He had given up his own room for her. After that, Ms. Farrell was careful never to complain to him about hotel accommodations.

**An Expensive Restaurant**

Mr. B's kindness was not an isolated event. When ballerina Darci Kistler first danced in a European tour with the New York City Ballet, she walked into a Paris restaurant and then discovered that it was much too expensive for her. She was very embarrassed and didn't know what to do, but fortunately Mr. Balanchine saw her and invited her to eat with him and his friends. Of course, Mr. Balanchine picked up the check.

**Taking the Wrong Train—Deep into Russia**

Robert Ivey, a dancer, once was in Krakow, Poland, but he needed to go to Warsaw and then take a train to Gdansk. He didn't speak the language, and he ended up taking the wrong train—he wasn't going toward Gdansk, but was going in the opposite direction, deep into Russia. He decided to get off at the next station and take the train heading in the right direction the next morning, so the train stopped at a tiny station, and he stepped out into the freezing Russian winter. The station was closed, but a Russian woman and her son appeared to pick up a few packages. Mr. Ivey spoke to them, hoping to at least be able to stay in the station, but he frightened them at first—then they smiled and said, "English!" Unfortunately, that was the only English word they knew, but they did say "Zimmer," which means "room" in German. Mr. Ivey stayed that night in the one-room home of the Russian woman and her family, who treated him well, cleaning his clothes, polishing his boots, and even giving him a precious egg for breakfast. Mr. Ivey rewarded them for their kindness in offering hospitality to him when he needed it. He gave the father his watch, the sons some of his shirts and sweaters, the mother a scarf and gloves, plus he gave them all his traveling allowance of Polish money and $30 in American money. Mr. Ivey never knew his hosts' names, but he has never forgotten them.

**Being Kind to Fans**

Fans waited in long lines to attend performances by ballet dancers Rudolf Nureyev and Margot Fonteyn. One day, while rehearsing *Romeo and Juliet*, Ms. Fonteyn saw a long line of fans waiting in the rain to get tickets, and she told Mr. Nureyev, "Rudolf, it's dreadful outside. I'm going to the canteen and bring those poor fans some coffee and doughnuts. They must be soaked to the skin!" Mr. Nureyev replied, "Margot, fans be happier with you if you stay here and rehearse and make perfect performance." She did stay and rehearse, but once rehearsal was over, she carried hot drinks to the fans waiting in the rain.

**Doing Good to People Who Do Bad**

Ballerina Illaria Obidenna Ladré liked to do something good to people who had done something bad to her. When Ms. Ladré wished to dance in Sergei Diaghilev's *Ballets Russes*, another dancer told Mr. Diaghilev that Ms. Ladré was probably a Bolshevik (a Communist in the Russian Revolution). This made Ms. Ladré very angry because she was nothing of the kind. However, as a kindness, when World War II started, she helped the dancer and her family reach safety in the United States.

**A Worthless Note of Brazilian Currency**

While in Brazil, ballet dancer H. Algeranoff made a purchase and then tried to pay for it with a Brazilian note he had received a few weeks earlier. Unfortunately, the note was worthless, having been taken out of circulation years earlier. The Brazilian shopkeeper was outraged that this trick had been played on a visitor, so he took Mr. Algeranoff and the note to a bank and managed to get the note exchanged for a good one.

**Buying a Pair of Slippers**

While traveling with dancer Anna Pavlova in Japan, music director Theodore Stier went into a Japanese shop to buy a pair of slippers. Slippers were not available in that particular shop, so the Japanese proprietor tried to explain where Mr. Stier could go to purchase them. Unfortunately, because of language difficulties, the two could not communicate well. Therefore, the Japanese proprietor left his shop and walked a mile and a half with Mr. Stier, guiding him to a shop that had slippers for sale.

**"A Gift from Rose"**

In Switzerland, the mother of dancer Ariane Pulver became aware of a Spanish family who had fled from the Spanish Civil War and was destitute. To help the family, she would fill a basket with food, put it on the doorstep along with a note saying "A gift from Rose," ring the doorbell, and leave. She did this for a long time, anonymously (the family did not know who Rose was). Later, the fortunes of this family rose, and its head became the Spanish consul in Switzerland. During World War II, Ariane's boyfriend, Paul Szilard, needed help because his Hungarian passport was not of much help to him in Switzerland. Ariane and Paul needed visas—Switzerland had decided to expel its foreigners, of whom Paul was one. At this time, Ariane's mother wrote a note to the Spanish consul. The note said, "Do you remember Rose? That's who writes you this letter. I would like to ask you for a favor. Will you help my daughter and her friend get a visa?" The next day, a basket of flowers arrived at her door, and the Spanish consul arranged for the visas and a way out of Switzerland for the young couple.

**Advice from a Friend, and a Letter to a Teacher**

When ballerina Chan Hon Goh was a little girl, she emigrated from China to Canada, where she did not fit in with the other children right away. On the playground during recess, the other children did not play with her because she was the only child of Chinese ancestry. In addition, because she did not know English well, some children called her "Retard" as well as "Chink." Finally, she told her father what was happening at school. He took action after consulting a friend of his, a musician in the Vancouver Symphony. Together, her father and the musician friend wrote a letter to her teacher, who did not know what was happening. Chan carried the letter to her teacher, who read it and then gave her a "warm and kind look" that reassured her. The teacher then left to talk to the children in the playground, and after that Chan was treated much nicer. In a few years, she learned English well and fit in with the other students.

### Paying for a Friend's Funeral

Coco Chanel earned a lot of money through her fashion design, the manufacture of costume jewelry, and the sales of her perfume, Chanel No. 5. She used that money in part to support the arts; for example, when dance impresario Sergei Diaghilev presented the ground-breaking ballet *Le Sacre du Printemps* (*The Rite of Spring*), the "angel" behind the production was Ms. Chanel, who provided the money for it secretly. One might expect that Mr. Diaghilev, a truly major force in the field of dance, would die with much money in the bank, but he died penniless. It was Ms. Chanel who generously paid for her friend's funeral.

### Segregation

During the Jim Crow days of segregated theaters, modern dance pioneer Martha Graham performed at all-black Spelman College. Afterward, she said that she would see some of the students at her performance in a public theater that evening. However, the black students explained that because of segregation, they would not be allowed to attend her performance there. Martha Graham grew angry, and it was never wise to go against the wishes of an angry Martha Graham. She saw the manager of the theater where she was to perform, and she gave him an ultimatum. Either the manager would set aside 20 seats for the students of Spelman College, or she would cancel her performance. The students got their seats.

### Stopping Evictions

The great dancer Bill Robinson, aka Mr. Bojangles, was known for his acts of charity. While walking on the street, he would sometimes see a family being evicted from their apartment. If he had the money—and he frequently did—he would pay the family's back rent, hire people to take the family's possessions back to the apartment, and buy groceries for the family.

### Dancing Courtesy

Fred Astaire and Audrey Hepburn worked together in the filming of *Funny Face*, and Ms. Hepburn was nervous about dancing with Mr. Astaire. The first dance they did together, Ms. Hepburn made a mistake, and they had to start over. During their second attempt, Ms. Hepburn made another mistake and again they had to start over. During their third attempt, Ms. Hepburn made yet another mistake—so Mr. Astaire immediately made a mistake of his own and then said, "Oh, I'm so sorry. I've ruined it. Can we do it again?" Mr. Astaire was such a good actor that Ms. Hepburn didn't know that he had deliberately made the mistake in order to save her from embarrassment.

# Chapter 7: TV AND MOVIES

**Kindness Toward Guest Stars**

Suzanne Pleshette, who played Emily Hartley, Bob's wife, on *The Bob Newhart Show*, had made a number of guest appearances on other TV series in the past, and so she realized the difficulty of being a guest star. After all, the guest star is going to be around for only one week, while the regulars on the series have already bonded and become a "family." Therefore, she always made an effort to make the guest stars on *The Bob Newhart Show* feel comfortable. She would let them know where the bathrooms were and who the assistant director was, and she would tell them that the regulars went to lunch together and if the guest star wanted to join them, he or she was welcome. Later, some of the guest stars had their own series and did what Ms. Pleshette did to make their guest stars comfortable. Ms. Pleshette says, "I was very proud when Henry Winkler [star of *Happy Days*] and John Ritter [star of *Three's Company*] both told me that they did the same things when they had their own shows because I had done it for them and it made a difference. And it does make a difference."

**"I Needed Clothes and You Clothed Me"**

One of the most valued mentors of TV's Mister Rogers was Dr. William Orr, a professor who taught theology at the seminary that Mister Rogers attended. One cold day, Dr. Orr put on an overcoat and went out to eat lunch. When he returned, he was not wearing the overcoat. Although Mister Rogers asked him about the overcoat, all Dr. Orr would say was that he had another overcoat at home—he would not tell Mister Rogers that he had given away his overcoat to someone who had needed it.

**Toast Sticks**

When TV's Mister Rogers was a young child, he sometimes visited a neighbor, Mama Bell Frampton, who gave him his favorite food: toast sticks. This treat consisted of slices of toast cut into pieces and smeared with butter and jam. One day, Mama Bell asked young Fred if he wanted to learn to make toast sticks. This was a big event for him. They made the toast in the toaster, and she let him smear butter and jam on the toast and then cut it into four "sticks." Decades later, whenever Mister Rogers heard "Love your neighbor as yourself," he thought of Mama Bell.

### The Murder of a Child

As a child, Oprah Winfrey was raped and suffered child abuse. In 1991, she was outraged by the murder of four-year-old Angelica Mena in Chicago, who was molested and then strangled. She said later, "I did not know the child, never heard her laughter. But I vowed that night to do something, to take a stand for the children of this country." Being rich and powerful has its advantages. She hired attorney and former Illinois governor James Thompson to draft a law to help protect children from molesters. The bill created a national registry of convicted child molesters and made it available to schools and child care centers so that they would not unknowingly hire a child molester. After the bill had been drafted, Delaware Senator Joseph Biden, a Democrat, sponsored it. Ms. Winfrey testified before the Senate Judiciary Committee about the abuse that she had suffered as a child, and the bill—nicknamed the "Oprah bill"—became enacted into law.

### Nickels in the Mail

In September of 1954, during his *Garry Moore Show*, Mr. Moore decided to do an act of kindness on the spur of the moment. He picked a young lady named Mrs. Charles Deibel out of his studio audience, introduced her to his TV audience, and asked his viewers to each send her a nickel. He also gave viewers an address in her hometown of Mt. Pleasant, Michigan, to mail the money. In less than 24 hours, over 8,000 letters arrived, and for a few days, 40,000 letters a day were arriving. By the time the avalanche of letters had stopped, Mrs. Deibel had received over 200,000 letters and over $12,000, much of it in nickels. The Internal Revenue Service announced that since the money consisted of small gifts and was not earned, it was 100 percent tax free.

### Fired Because of Moonlighting

Garry Moore, a star of early television, was a kind man. One day, he heard that a black man named Marshall, who worked as a janitor in his studio, had been fired because he was moonlighting. Furious, Mr. Moore got Marshall his job back. Marshall thanked him, saying, "'Cause you know, Mr. Moore, show business is my life."

### Money for College

*Let's Make a Deal* game-show host Monty Hall grew up in an impoverished family. Although he was very intelligent, attending college did not seem to be an option for him until a man who was thought to be a playboy met him, was impressed by his intelligence, and wondered why he was delivering packages for a living. The playboy offered to pay his way through college on five conditions: "Number one, I want you to keep an A average. Number two, I want you to pay back every penny. Number three, I want you to report to me every month. Number four, I want you to do this for someone else some day. Number five, never tell anyone where you got the dough [money]." Mr. Hall graduated in 1945 from the University of Manitoba.

**Famous Fone Friends**

Nancy Cartwright, the voice of TV's Bart Simpson, participates in Famous Fone Friends, an organization in which celebrities telephone children who have cancer or are otherwise seriously ill. One day, Ms. Cartwright telephoned a boy who was so ill that he was unable to speak. She used Bart's voice to talk to him for about five minutes—until his mother got on the telephone to say that her son was so excited that he needed a little oxygen to calm down!

**"It's Mine No More Than Hers"**

Actor/writer/director Paul Bern often gave money to the poor. One day, an impoverished woman waited in his office to see him. Because he was busy, he sent her some money and a note of apology for being unable to see her. He also told a friend about the money: "It's mine no more than hers."

***Crossover Dreams***

Hispanic actor Rubén Blades made the movie *Crossover Dreams*, about a salsa singer who wants to make it big by crossing over into pop music. The all-Hispanic movie, made by a small film company called Max Mambru, was filmed in East Harlem, where residents brought the actors and production crew soup. To show their appreciation for the soup, the actors and crew painted the homes of several East Harlem good-deed doers. Mr. Blades points out, "Everybody in the community cooperated. It was a Latin effort done by ourselves to help ourselves."

**A Hungry Chorus Girl**

Boxer Jim Tully once saw actor Clark Gable give a hungry chorus girl $20 and then cover her mouth with his hand so she couldn't thank him.

**Too Proud to Take Money from Her Son**

Walter Matthau's mother was proud and wouldn't take presents of money from him, so he had to figure out a way to give her money. Finally, he started taking her to the dog races. He would bet money for her, and she would take home the winnings. Mr. Matthau's dog-picking ability was amazing—he was able to pick the winner of every race, and so his mother always came home with lots of money after going with him to the dog races. But what Mr. Matthau didn't tell his mother was that he would bet on every dog in the race, put each betting ticket in a different pocket (memorizing which pocket had which betting ticket), and whatever dog won, he would reach into the pocket that held the winning ticket, hand the ticket to his mother, and have her collect the winnings.

**What Should a Caring Boyfriend Do?**

After making the movie *Scream 2*, Sarah Michelle Gellar, star of TV's *Buffy the Vampire Slayer*, spent so much time promoting the movie that she felt stressed and did not eat properly. What should a caring boyfriend do? Freddie Prinze, Jr., and a bunch of his friends invaded Sarah's kitchen, cooked a feast, and then left her refrigerator very well stocked indeed. (And yes, Sarah and Freddie got married later.)

**"We Don't Have Any Dolls"**

On an outing, Eunice and her Aunt Elsie noticed two little girls eagerly looking at two dolls in a store window. The little girls were poorly dressed, a fact which Aunt Elsie noticed immediately. Aunt Elsie spoke to the two little girls, asking them about the dolls, which the little girls praised extravagantly. Aunt Elsie then asked, "Are these dolls as pretty as the dolls you have at home?" The older of the two girls replied, "We don't have any dolls. We have never had any dolls." Aunt Elsie immediately bought the little girls the dolls they had been admiring in the store window.

**Maid of Honor**

Aunt Elsie's Eunice was Eunice Quedens, who grew up to become the famous radio, TV, and movie star Eve Arden, but who never forgot the lesson she had learned from Aunt Elsie. These days, television and movie celebrities tend to be wary about accepting invitations from fans—because of a few weirdoes, they have good reason to be wary. However, occasionally a celebrity will accept an invitation with very good results. As the star of the TV sitcom *Our Miss Brooks*, featuring the title character of an often sarcastic but always lovable teacher, Ms. Arden was a major celebrity. Because she appeared on TV in so many fans' homes every week, lots of people—especially teachers—felt that they knew her. One of the fan letters Ms. Arden received was from a

Chicago teacher whom she had never met, inviting her to be the maid of honor at the woman's wedding. Ms. Arden discretely investigated the writer of the letter, discovered that she was not a weirdo, accepted the invitation, and made a new friend.

# Chapter 8: THEATER

**"Hang Them"**

Although Percy Hammond was feared because of the sharpness of his drama criticism, he sometimes did kindnesses for other journalists. When Whitney Bolton was new to New York City and feeling very out of place, Mr. Hammond gave him two tickets to a musical comedy and said, "It's not that tough a town, kid. Take these and have some fun. You look as though you need it." After Mr. Bolton had worked his way up from copy boy to novice drama critic and was attending his first play, Mr. Hammond noticed how nervous he was, so he wrote a note on his program and gave it to him: "They're just actors. If you don't like them, hang them. Never mind what the rest of us think. Do it your way."

**A Famous Tour Guide**

On her first day on the job at the National Theatre, Jane Suffling didn't know anyone. She wandered into the canteen, where an elderly gentleman wearing carpet slippers asked if she were new. She confessed that she was and that she felt lost, so he said, "Oh, that must be terrible for you. Let me show you around." He then took her all over the theater, showing her the rehearsal rooms, wig room, and so on. The next day he passed her and spoke to her—and her colleagues were in awe. After he had gone, they asked Ms. Suffling, "How do you know him? Where have you worked with him before?" She admitted, "I only met him yesterday, and he showed me all over the building." She also admitted that she didn't know his name, so they told her that her kindly guide had been the famous actor Sir Ralph Richardson.

**"This is What I am Really Like"**

*"L'Aiglon"* ("Eaglet") was a nickname for Napoleon II, son of Napolean I and his second wife. Edmond Rostand wrote a play titled *L'Aiglon* that the great actress Sarah Bernhardt starred in. She played the character L'Aiglon so convincingly that a young woman fell in love with her and refused to see young men. After Ms. Bernhardt learned of the infatuation, she asked that the admirer be sent to her, and she received the young woman in her dressing room while she was wearing an old bathrobe and no makeup. She told her admirer, "This is what I am really like. There is no such person as L'Aiglon except on the stage."

The young woman married and had a baby—Ms. Bernhardt was the child's godmother.

### "You Can Do This"

Patti Colombo went to New York City to break into dancing, did not break in, and came back home to Marin County, California, where she tried somehow to fit dancing into her life. When *A Chorus Line* came to San Francisco, where it was (of course) a huge hit, Ms. Colombo determined to become a member of the cast. She attended an open audition and performed well until it was time to do a triple turn, which she could always do in class but became too nervous to do in the audition. Michael Bennett, co-choreographer of *A Chorus Line*, saw her and said, "Patti, you can do this. Now do it." Thinking to herself, "God, he knew my name," she did a triple turn—and won the role of Val.

### An Advance Royalty Check

Theatrical director Tyrone Guthrie once had his theatrical company send a book contract and an advance royalty check of £200 to an actress. The actress wrote back, "Thank you very much for your letter and very kind cheque. I've signed the contract, because I know and love you, but can't understand what it's all about, because I should never dream of writing a book in my life." That's how the employees who had written the book contract discovered that this was merely Mr. Guthrie's way of giving the actress a much-needed £200.

### A Troubled Man Gazing Into a River

Frank Rodney, a British theatrical romantic lead in the late 19th century, once saw a troubled man gazing into a river. Struck by the sadness in the man's face, Mr. Rodney spoke to him and soon learned that the man had embezzled money from his employer and could not repay it. Because of this, he was thinking of committing suicide. Mr. Rodney gave him enough money to cover his debt, after first making the man promise to go straight. The man did go straight and afterward became an honest businessman.

# Chapter 9: EDUCATION

**"Happy Birthday"**

A big deal in kindergarten is to have a birthday because all the other children sing "Happy Birthday" to you. One little girl was sad because her birthday was in July, which meant that her classmates would never sing "Happy Birthday" to her. One day, the little girl went to her kindergarten teacher and said that it was her birthday. Although the teacher knew that the little girl's birthday was really in July, she had the little girl's classmates sing "Happy Birthday" to her.

**Bringing Color to a Beige World**

In St. Croix, U.S. Virgin Islands, Carol Hole was the librarian of a kindergarten-to-eighth-grade school that had been painted in dreary shades of grey, brown, and beige. Due to a lack of school funding, Ms. Hole and art teacher Marina Pukinsikis used their own money to do what they could to bring color into such a dreary place. In the hallway were a few display cases, and they decided to paint them bright orange and then put in them artwork by the students. After they had finished painting a display case, a seven-year-old boy walked by them. He did a doubletake, walked back to the display case, waved and said, "HELLO, ORANGE!" Then he walked off with a big smile on his face.

**Milk Money**

In 1940, children's book author/illustrator Tomie dePaola was in Mrs. Kiniry's first-grade class. Each day, Mrs. Kiniry read the names of all the children who had brought in their dime for their milk that week, and each day Mrs. Kiniry read the names of all the children in the class. (Actually, not all the children had a dime for their milk, and Mr. dePaola discovered later that Mrs. Kiniry used her own money to pay for the milk so that everyone could have milk and no one would be embarrassed because their name was not read.)

**Free College—Followed by Free Law School**

Constance Baker, a young African-American woman, spoke out when Clarence W. Blakeslee held a meeting to find out why a community center he had donated to the African-American community was not being used very much. Ms. Baker pointed out that no African Americans were on the community center board of directors and so African Americans felt as if they had no say—or interest—in the center. Mr. Blakeslee was impressed by what she said, so he looked into her background. He even met with her in his office and asked why she wasn't in college, since her educational background showed that she was clearly capable of it. She lacked money, so she couldn't afford to go to college, but Mr. Blakeslee paid her way through college—and then he paid her way through law school. Ms. Baker, who married and took the name Constance Baker Motley, became the first woman lawyer to work for the National Association for the Advancement of Colored People. One of the cases she worked on ended up in the Supreme Court: *Brown v. Topeka, Kansas, Board of Education.*

**Getting in Trouble with Sign Language**

Michelle Smithdas lost her hearing due to a congenital defect, and she lost her sight due to an automobile accident. Helping her get a master's degree at Columbia Teachers College was Linda Stillman, who finger spelled lectures into Michelle's palm. (This was the same technique that Annie Sullivan and Helen Keller used.) While sitting in class, Ms. Stillman would sometimes tell (using finger spelling) Ms. Smithdas what the other students were wearing, or she would tell jokes. Occasionally, teachers reprimanded Ms. Smithdas for laughing loudly during class.

# Chapter 10: FAMILY AND FRIENDS

**Emperor of the United States**

Joshua Abraham Norton, an Englishman, moved to the United States in 1849. Living in San Francisco, he owned his own business and did well financially until he was wiped out by a bad investment. Apparently, the financial loss drove him crazy, as on Sept. 17, 1859, he walked into the office of the *San Francisco Bulletin* with a declaration stating that at the "request of and desire of a large majority of the citizens of these United States, I, Joshua Abraham Norton, ... declare and proclaim myself emperor of these United States." Amused by the declaration, the editor printed it on the front page and Mr. Norton became Emperor Norton I.

The people of San Francisco liked the emperor. To get money to live on, Emperor Norton I walked into businesses and levied a "tax" on them; the business owners knew that the money would go straight to the emperor's pockets but they paid it anyway. (Small businesses paid a quarter; large businesses paid a dollar or two.) The emperor would sometimes ask a loyal subject for a loan of several hundred million dollars; these requests for loans were always turned down, but the emperor cheerfully accepted the gift of a dime in the place of the loan. Emperor Norton I often walked into restaurants, where he expected to eat for free—and where he did eat for free. His loving subjects paid his streetcar fares and his laundry bills. The Central Pacific Railroad did its part to support the emperor by giving him a free lifetime pass to all of its dining and sleeping cars in California. The San Francisco Board of Supervisors did its part to support the emperor by voting—unanimously—to pay for a new suit of royal clothing.

After being emperor for 21 years, Norton I died, and the entire city of San Francisco went into mourning for him. His loyal subjects paid $10,000 for his funeral, and 8,000 people came to view him in his casket. An obituary for Emperor Norton I stated, "The Emperor Norton killed nobody, robbed nobody and deprived nobody of his country—which is more than can be said for most fellows in his trade."

**"A Hot Dog on a Bun"**

A mother, a father, and their small daughter were sitting in a restaurant. The waitress asked for the parents' order and then asked the small child what she wanted. The child said, "A hot dog on a bun." The mother said, "No hot dog. She'll have chicken." The father added, "With mashed potatoes and vegetables." The waitress ignored the parents and asked the child, "Would you like ketchup or mustard on your hot dog?" The child said, "Mustard, please." The waitress said, "Coming right up," and left to get their orders. The parents were stunned, but the child said, "You know what? She treats me like a real person!"

**Smuggling a Puppy**

After 16-year-old Joni Eareckson broke her neck while diving into shallow water, she was paralyzed and had to spend months suspended in a Stryker frame. One day Dick, her boyfriend, came to visit her. Oddly, he was wearing a jacket on a very warm day and he had climbed nine flights of stairs instead of taking an elevator to get to Joni's Intensive Care Unit. However, Joni understood why Dick had done these things when he opened his jacket and took out the puppy he had smuggled into the hospital. The puppy licked Joni's face, and they played with it for an hour. Eventually, they got caught by an on-duty nurse who asked about the puppy, "How'd you get him past the Gestapo in the lobby?" Dick explained that he had taken the stairs, and then he asked if she was going to turn him in. The nurse smiled, said, "Who? Me? I never saw a thing," then exited. (Nurses are kind people who do what is best for their patients. Sometimes, allowing a rule to be broken is better for a patient than enforcing the rules.) By the way, later this scene was filmed for a movie starring Joni, but a problem arose because the puppy used in the scene kept squirming and did everything but lick Joni's face. The filmmakers solved the problem by smearing liver-flavored baby food on one side of Joni's face—then the puppy enthusiastically licked the baby food for the scene.

**Notes in a Son's Lunchbox**

Christian writer Dale Hanson Bourke used to put notes—simple words or pictures—in her small son's lunchbox. This created a trend at her son's school, because Chase, her son, showed the notes to other children and their parents followed her example. At the end of each school day, Ms. Bourke would see her note in her son's lunchbox. By that time, the note would usually be smeared with the fingerprints of the children who had looked at it. One day, the note was missing, and she asked young Chase about it. Chase said, "Sorry, Mom. I gave it to Jimmy." She asked why, and Chase replied, "I hope you don't mind, Mom, but he never gets a note. So I thought I could share mine with him." Jimmy's Mom was a hard-working single mother with little time, so Ms. Bourke told her son, "You're a very special boy." He replied, "I know."

**Shoveling Snow**

After some friends had been volunteering at the Salvation Army, they piled into a car and started going to their various homes. As they drew near one of the men's homes, they saw an elderly woman shoveling snow. The man who lived nearby asked to be let off at the corner. Everyone thought that he merely wanted to walk the rest of the way to his house, but the driver of the car was unfamiliar with the neighborhood and after making a few wrong turns, began driving down the same street where the elderly woman had been shoveling snow. This time, the elderly woman was not shoveling her snow—the man who had asked to be dropped off was doing it for her.

**"We Love Him"**

In the 1850s, the United States lacked social services such as Welfare, Social Security, and Children Services. Often, families were poor and could not feed their children. Therefore, a man named Charles Loring Brace took action. He founded the Children's Aid Society to place poor children in homes in rural communities. The children rode a train and at each stop were displayed to farm families who could chose a child or two to live and work with them. The Society would send agents out periodically to make sure that the children were OK. One "problem" child was placed with a German. The agent visited after only three months instead of the usual six months because he was sure that the German couple would give the boy back to the Children's Aid Society. However, the German couple wanted to keep the boy. Genuinely surprised, the agent asked why. The German couple replied, "We love him."

**Pawning Her Rings**

Thurgood Marshall wanted to attend the Howard University Law School in Washington, D.C., but he faced the problem of not having enough money. However, his mother, Norma, told him, "You're going. I'll pawn my engagement and wedding rings to help you." She did pawn her rings, and she never saw them again. Mr. Marshall not only graduated from law school, but in 1952 and 1953 he successfully argued *Brown v. Board of Education* before the Supreme Court, striking down the doctrine of "separate but equal," and in

1967, President Lyndon Johnson appointed him to the United States Supreme Court.

# Chapter 11: CHRISTMAS

**A Bushel of Apples**

Hyrum Smith is the chair of the Franklin Quest Company, makers of organizational planners. While he was growing up on one of the Hawaiian islands, his parents felt that one Christmas would be bleak because of lack of money. However, they told their children that they could ask for one gift. To their surprise, Hyrum asked for a bushel of apples, which were rare on the Hawaiian islands. When Christmas came, Hyrum received his bushel of apples and then experienced the joy of giving as he delivered apples to his friends and neighbors.

**Warm Coats and Cappuccinos**

Because of Barney Pressman, who started Barneys in New York City, hundreds of needy children did not need a warm coat because he gave away hundreds of warm coats each Christmas. He was also very good at getting other people to contribute to charity. During the 1960s, he persuaded some stewardesses—whom Barneys window dresser Simon Doonan calls "the supermodels of their day"—to serve cappuccinos at his store. Young men came by to look at the pretty women and buy cappuccinos, the proceeds of which went to charity. (No fool, Mr. Pressman also convinced many of the young men to buy a suit.)

**Something More Meaningful**

After Pop artist Andy Warhol said that he wanted to do something more meaningful with his life, he started spending Easter and Christmas with his friend Paige Powell serving meals at a church soup kitchen. He enjoyed this in part because none of the people there knew who he was.

**A Nobody's Fool Christmas Dinner**

At the very beginning of her career, opera singer/actress Grace Moore spent a penniless Christmas in New York City. She had been invited to eat a Christmas dinner with a Mr. Ginsberg, who was serving turkey cooked by the famous chef Arnold Reuben; however, she decided that she would rather not eat Christmas dinner than eat it with strangers. Nevertheless, eating a Christmas dinner was better than not eating a Christmas dinner, so she used her wits and telephoned the famous Mr. Reuben, saying that she was a friend of Mr. Ginsberg, she was newly arrived in New York, she had no cash on her because the banks had closed, and could he please send her a dinner on credit. The famous Mr. Reuben, of course, was no fool, but it was Christmas, and Christmas is a time of good deeds, and so he sent her a huge dinner on credit—she and her friends dined for days on the leftovers. When Ms. Moore much later made her opera debut in New York City, sitting in a box was the famous chef—and personal friend of Ms. Moore—Mr. Reuben.

**A Win-Win Christmas Dinner**

When Ernestine Schumann-Heink was a young, struggling opera singer, she was faced with an upcoming hungry, bleak Christmas. Fortunately, another opera singer, Matilda Brandt, knew her situation, and since Ms. Brandt was separated from her husband that Christmas because they were working in different cities, she came up with a win-win proposal for Ms. Schumann-Heink: Ms. Brandt would buy the food for Christmas dinner, and Ms. Schumann-Heink would cook it. Together, they had a wonderful Christmas dinner, and Ms. Schumann-Heink kept and enjoyed the leftovers.

# Chapter 12: HOLOCAUST

**Rhetoric in a Death Camp**

In May 1941, Maximilian Kolbe, a Catholic priest, was sent to Auschwitz. After a prisoner escaped, the Nazis chose ten prisoners to be sent to the starvation bunker to die a slow death in retaliation for the one prisoner who had escaped. One of the ten prisoners picked out to die begged for mercy, saying that he had a wife and children. Fr. Kolbe, who had no wife and children, volunteered to die in that man's place. To convince the Nazis to agree to the switch, he made the persuasive points that he was older than the other man and that the other man was in better shape to work for the Nazis than he was. The Nazis agreed to let him die instead of the other man, and on 15 August 1941, Fr. Kolbe's corpse was burned in a crematorium along with the corpses of the other nine men. On 10 October 1982, Pope John Paul II consecrated him a saint.

**"I Cannot Allow These People to Die"**

One of the rescuers of Jews during the Holocaust was Sempo Sugihara, the Japanese diplomat to Lithuania. While in Lithuania's capital, Mr. Sugihara issued visas to thousands of Jews that allowed them to leave Lithuania and travel through Japan to other countries where they would be safe. In issuing the visas, Mr. Sugihara at first acted without orders. He had asked his government for permission to issue the visas, but when he did not receive an answer, he thought, "I cannot allow these people to die—people who have come to me for help with death staring them in the eyes. Whatever punishment may be imposed on me, I know I should follow my conscience." Later, he received direct orders not to issue the visas, but he continued to issue them anyway. He kept the Japanese consulate open late at night, and a line of Jews formed outside the consulate. Some nights Mr. Sugihara's hands were so stiff from writing visas that he could not move them until his wife had massaged them. Eventually, he was forced to leave Lithuania, but at the train station and even while the train was chugging out of the station, he was writing visas and handing them out the window.

**A Very Non-Kosher Meal**

A Polish farmer hid cantor Isaac Goodfriend during the Holocaust. After the war, they separated, but he later returned with some observant Jews to visit the farmer, who was very glad to see him. The farmer prepared the table for a meal with his guests, setting down such items as slices of ham. Mr. Goodfriend's friends were amused by the very non-kosher meal, but he told them that although the farmer knew little about Judaism, he knew an enormous amount about human kindness and decency.

**Trying Unsuccessfully to be Served**

During the 1930s, Arnold Douwes of the Netherlands sat down in a restaurant in Chicago, where he noticed a black man trying unsuccessfully to be served. Mr. Douwes talked to the black man and learned about the discrimination that was then common in the United States. When his own meal came, he gave it to the black man and ordered another meal. For this, he was arrested. His altruism didn't stop there. During World War II, Mr. Douwes and a network of 250 other people in the town of Nieuwlande saved the lives of thousands of Jews.

**"We Must Obey God Before We Obey Man"**

In October of 1943, the Nazis were preparing to deport all Jews from the country of Denmark. H. Fuglsand-Damgaard, the Lutheran bishop of Copenhagen, urged all Danes to resist the Nazi effort, saying, "We must obey God before we obey man." Thousands of lay people agreed, and the Danes used their fishing boats to help 7,720 Jews escape to Sweden. A total of 464 Danish Jews did not escape and were deported to the Theresienstadt concentration camp, but the Danish government kept up pressure on their behalf and only 51 died before the war ended—a small number and percentage in comparison with the deaths of other groups of Jews in the concentration camps.

**Outwitting the Nazis**

During World War II, the Danes saved many Jews by sailing them from Denmark to Sweden. The Nazis realized that the Danes' fishing boats must have hidden compartments, so they began using specially trained dogs to sniff out the Jews. These dogs were so gifted that they could smell the Jews even after they had been hidden and a load of fish had been dumped over the entrance to their hiding place. Therefore, Swedish scientists developed a way to keep the dogs from sniffing out the Jews. They created a powder made of dried rabbit blood and cocaine. The dried blood attracted the dogs, and when they sniffed it, the cocaine dulled their sense of smell. Danish fishermen began to carry handkerchiefs contaminated with the powder. When the Nazis came around with their dogs, the fishermen would find a way to let the dogs sniff their handkerchiefs, perhaps by "accidentally" dropping them on the ground. This trick saved the lives of many Jews and many Resistance members.

**Bringing Water to the Thirsty**

During World War II in Hungary, many Jews were forced to endure "death marches"—they were made to march long distances to places where they were supposed to do slave labor, even though the Nazis and their supporters knew that many of the Jews would die before reaching the end of the march. Some Hungarians helped when they could. Miriam Herzog marched along the road to Hegyeshalom, and a Hungarian man carried water to thirsty Jews, including Ms. Herzog. Members of the anti-Semitic military group the Arrow Cross tried to stop him, but he refused to be intimidated. She says, "The gendarmes tried to stop him, but he just fixed them with a stare. 'I'd like to see you try to make me,' he said—and went on giving us water. The gendarmes were so amazed, they did nothing about it."

**Spunk at a Wedding and During War**

Alice, Princess Andrew of Greece, had spunk. When she got married to Prince Andrew in 1903, Czar Nicholas II of Russia threw rice a little too hard at her. Annoyed, she took off one of her shoes and hit him with it. Later, she used her spunk to hide a Jewish family and save them from the Holocaust, for which she was named one of the Righteous among the Nations, just like Oskar Schindler.

# Chapter 13: RABBIS

**Wine and Meat**

Just before Passover, a man came to ask Rabbi Chaim of Volozin, "May I substitute four glasses of milk for the four cups of wine which it is customary to drink in the Passover eve ceremony?" The rabbi asked if the man wanted to do this because the man was ill and the wine would not be good for him. Hearing that the man was in good health but impoverished, the rabbi gave him five rubles and told him to buy some wine and celebrate Passover Eve. After the man had joyfully gone, the rabbi's wife asked him why he had given the man so much money; after all, two rubles would have been enough to purchase the necessary wine. The rabbi explained that since the man had asked to substitute milk for the wine, the man must have also lacked money for meat because drinking milk and eating meat at the same meal is not kosher. Therefore, the rabbi had given the man enough money to buy both wine and meat.

**A Grocery Store**

Although the Chofetz Chaim, aka Rabbi Yisroel Meir Kagan, was a famous scholar, he ran a small grocery store to make a living. However, when he discovered that many people exclusively patronized his grocery store because of his reputation as a scholar, thus hurting the livelihood of other grocers in the area, he closed his grocery store.

**High-Rise Apartments**

Hasidic leader Rabbi Menachem Mendel Schneerson, aka the Lubavitcher Rebbe, once spoke to Rabbi Morris N. Kertzer and made a request of him. In New York City, some of his Hasidic followers were applying for apartments in high-rise apartments in Brooklyn, and he wanted Rabbi Kertzer to request of New York City officials that the Hasidic followers be given apartments on the first three floors of the high-rises. Why? According to traditional Jewish law, the Hasidic followers could not use the elevator on the Sabbath and on Jewish holy days.

**Loans for the Poor**

R' Zalman, the son of R' Uri of Vilna, often made interest-free loans to help other people. One day, a man he had never seen came to him to ask for a loan of 300 rubles for 90 days. R' Zalman asked who would be the guarantor of the loan; after all, he had never seen the man before. The man replied that he was new to the area, and so he had no friends there; therefore, Hashem was his only guarantor. R' Zalman said, "We can't ask for a better guarantor than that," then he wrote "He that has pity upon the poor lends to Hashem" (Mishlei 19:17). This he placed with the other documents he had received from people guaranteeing loans. Ninety days later, the man came to repay the loan, but R' Zalman said that the loan had already been repaid—the very day that he had made the loan he had concluded a business deal that made him exactly 300 rubles. However, the man insisted on repaying, and in the end they agreed that the money would be used for future loans to the poor and that the mitzvah would be shared by both of them.

### Honoring a Beggar

A poor man once asked Rabbi Boruch Ber Leibowitz for money. Unfortunately, the good rabbi lacked money, so he was unable to help the poor man monetarily. However, he did take a walk with the poor man, and when the good rabbi's students saw him walking with the poor man, they also joined in the walk. Although the poor man did not receive money, he was happy with the great honor that had been shown him. Later, Rabbi Leibowitz told his students, "A beggar humiliates himself because of the donation he expects to receive. If I am not able to give him money, at least I can give him honor."

### "Spit in My Eye"

A woman's husband was angry with Rabbi Meir, and he ordered his wife either to spit in Rabbi Meir's eye or be sent away in disgrace. Rabbi Meir found out what the woman's husband had ordered, so he pretended that something was wrong with his eye, and he requested that the woman help him fix his eye by following an old folk remedy—she should spit in his eye seven times.

### "Are Not Hearts Trumps?"

A young girl bore a note from her father to Rabbi Akiba Eger: "In my great distress I must appeal to you; there is not a piece of bread in my house. My wife and six children are almost dying of hunger, and I cannot find work. If I had as much money as a card player loses in a game at a gambling house, it would save me from distress." Rabbi Akiba lacked money, but to raise money for the act of charity, he went to a gambling house, went over to a card game where a lot of money was in the center of the table, and asked, "Tell me, are not hearts trumps?" Then he showed the note to the card players, who read it and told him, "You win, rabbi," and gave him the money for that hand.

**Thumbs Up**

During the glory and bloody days of the Roman Empire, crowds of Romans were entertained by the gladiatorial games at the Colosseum. This led to a dilemma for the Jews living in Rome. At the gladiatorial games, when one gladiator defeated another gladiator, the crowd would shout either "thumbs up" or "thumbs down." "Thumbs up" meant the gladiator would live; "thumbs down" meant the gladiator would die. Obviously, lots of deaths of human beings occurred in the Colosseum, and obviously, one ought not to take pleasure in the unnecessary death of another human being. Many rabbis declared that Jews ought not to attend the gladiatorial games; however, Rabbi Nathan disagreed. He felt that Jews ought to attend the gladiatorial games and shout "thumbs up," thus perhaps saving the life of a human being.

**Afraid of Dogs**

Rabbi Nochumke of Horodno had great compassion for other human beings. One day, a small boy, a member of his yeshiva (school), knocked on his door just as the good Rabbi and his family were sitting down to eat the Sabbath meal. With tears streaming down his face, the boy explained his problem: A large dog was in front of the door of the house where he was to eat, and he was afraid to go in. Rabbi Nochumke took the small boy by the hand, led him to the house, waited outside until the boy was done eating and then escorted the boy back to the yeshiva. Only then did he return to his house to eat with his family.

**A Suitcase of Money**

Before World War II, the Ponovezher Yeshiva (school) was located in Poland (it is now located in Israel), and its existence was threatened by a lack of money. The head of the yeshiva went to Rabbi Dr. Naftali Carlebach for help. They discussed the matter, and neither man noticed that the Rabbi's wife, Paula, had disappeared. When she returned, she was lugging a suitcase filled with money. As the two men had been discussing the problem, she had gone through the house, gathered up the valuables, and then taken them to a pawnbroker to get the money to save the yeshiva.

**Honor Thy Parents**

Rabbi Joseph Zundel believed in the commandment to honor thy parents. His mother used to get her feet dirty while walking through an unpaved alleyway on her way to the synagogue, so Rabbi Zundel paved the alleyway with his own hands.

**"Buy Fine Apples!"**

Rabbi Hayyim was in the marketplace one day when he heard a widow, who was selling apples, complaining about the poor business she was doing that day. Immediately, the good rabbi began shouting, "Buy fine apples!" The people of the village were astonished and came running to see Rabbi Hayyim sell apples, and the widow did good business that day.

# Chapter 14: RELIGION

**A Donkey-Driver**

In a dream, wise men saw a certain donkey-driver pray for rain, and rain fell immediately. The wise men sent for the donkey-driver and asked what good deed had he done. The donkey-driver replied that he had seen a woman crying in a street, and he had asked what was wrong. The woman told him that her husband was in prison, and that she would be forced to sell her body in order to get money to free him. So the donkey-driver sold one of his donkeys and gave the money to the woman to free her husband. After hearing this story, the wise men told the donkey-driver, "You are worthy to pray, and to be answered."

**Selling Cookies**

On 18 April 1966, fire broke out in the library of the Jewish Theological Seminary of America in New York City, destroying 85,000 books. Many people volunteered time and donated money to rescue the remaining 165,000 books, many of which were damaged by fire, smoke, and water. Children attending kindergarten at Riverside Church near the Jewish Theological Seminary of America even held a bake sale, selling cookies for five cents each and raising $62.65 that they donated to help save the books.

**Cultivating the Fruits of God's Bounty**

In 1950, a snowstorm devastated the crops of some Israeli farmers on the Sea of Galilee, but luckily for them their neighbors in Jordan—Arabs all—came through in a big way, giving them what was needed to plant a new crop. These Arab neighbors and the Israeli farmers worked together to cultivate the fruits of God's bounty.

**Cooperation**

In Ann Arbor, Michigan, is a building that serves as both a church (the St. Clare of Assisi Episcopal Church) and a synagogue (Temple Beth Emeth). On Yom Kippur and Rosh Hashanah, Christians babysit the children of the Jews. On Christmas and Easter, Jews babysit the children of the Christians.

**No Sweet Tea**

William Allen, a Quaker, was invited to have tea with Emperor Alexander of Russia. Mr. Allen tasted the tea, discovered that it was sweetened with sugar, and told the emperor that he could not drink it, as sugar was then harvested by slave labor. Emperor Alexander ordered unsweetened tea for Mr. Allen.

**"How Much Art Thou Sorry?"**

Jacob Bright, a Quaker, once came across a neighbor in distress. The neighbor's valuable beast of burden had met with an accident, forcing it to be destroyed. Around the neighbor were several people, all of whom were exclaiming how sorry they were about the accident. Mr. Bright listened for a few moments, and then he turned to a man who was loudly saying how sorry he was, and Mr. Bright said to him, "I'm sorry £5. How much art thou sorry?" Mr. Bright then collected money to help the neighbor in distress.

**"Friend, I Have Not a Cent in the World"**

Thomas Garrett, a Quaker, was a fervent abolitionist. Once he was caught helping a slave woman and her child escape to freedom, and he was taken before a judge. The judge knew that Mr. Garrett was a man of his word, and he offered to let Mr. Garrett go free if he would give his word not to help any more runaway slaves. Mr. Garrett responded, "Friend, thee better proceed with thy business." He was given a jury trial, found guilty, and was fined $8,000—a lot of money now, but a huge amount of money before the Civil War. In fact, the fine, combined with business problems, made him bankrupt. After the trial, Mr. Garrett told the sheriff, "Friend, I have not a cent in the world, but if thee knows of a man needing a meal, send him to me."

**Money for People, Not Buildings**

Quakers are involved in various relief efforts. Once, a non-Quaker driver was helping to transport relief goods from one Quaker meetinghouse to another. He looked at the plain interiors of the meetinghouses—no altar, no stained glass windows, etc.—and said, "These Quakers spend money for people, instead of buildings."

**Conductor of the Underground Railroad**

As a conductor of the Underground Railroad, Harriet Tubman, herself an escaped slave, led other escaped slaves from safe house to safe house until they reached freedom. Once, she took a group of people to what was supposed to be a safe house, but inside was a stranger who ordered them to leave. Afraid that the stranger would alert the authorities, Ms. Tubman hid herself and the escaped slaves in the tall grass of a swamp, and they spent the day there, afraid and hungry. After they had been hidden for several hours, a Quaker walked along the edge of the swamp. He didn't look into the swamp, but he did repeat over and over in a soft voice the location of his wagon and horse. Ms. Tubman and the escaped slaves took the wagon and horse and traveled to the next safe house. There she gave the wagon and horse to a trusted person so they could be returned to the Quaker.

### Two Sets of Invisible Sutras

Tetsugen was a Zen master who wished to publish in Japanese some religious writings known as the sutras—which in his day were available only in Chinese. To fund the publishing of the sutras, he traveled for 10 years, giving lectures and collecting donations. Finally, he had enough money to begin publishing the sutras. However, a flood occurred, which was followed by famine. Tetsugen took the money he had collected and used it to buy food to feed starving people. Again, he began collecting money for the publication of the sutras. Unfortunately, an epidemic occurred, and once again Tetsugen helped the people with the money he had collected. For the third time, he collected money, and finally he was able to publish the sutras. According to the Japanese, Tetsugen published not one—but three—sets of sutras. The most beautiful sets he published were the first two sets, which were invisible.

### Hitting the Shopkeeper Again

A young woman seeker after truth took up meditation with a Zen master and tried to fill her mind with lovingkindness for all human beings. However, on a rainy day she was sexually harassed by a shopkeeper, so she took her umbrella and hit the shopkeeper. Just then, the Zen master entered the shop. The woman immediately realized that she had forgotten all about lovingkindness, but the Zen master told her to fill her heart with lovingkindness and then hit the shopkeeper again.

### Good Advice from the Buddha

According to the Buddha, if you are angry at someone, you should give that person a gift. The mother of a student was furious at him for traveling to India to practice Buddhism. In a letter to him, she wrote, "I would rather see you in hell than where you are now." Dipa Ma, his meditation teacher, often asked the student how his mother was and whether during meditation he was sending lovingkindness to her. One day, she even gave the student 100 rupees (at the time, about $12, a lot of money to her) and told him to buy his mother a gift.

### An Exhausted Bird

A Buddhist monk was walking on a road when an exhausted bird fell into his hands. The monk said, "It seems the Bodhisatwa has sent me this bird to take care of." However, the bird recovered and flew away. The monk then said, "It seems the Bodhisatwa wanted me to do a good deed and release a living soul."

**Praying for a Dead Man's Soul**

According to *The Bild* in Hamburg, Germany, a Spanish Roman Catholic named Eduardo Sierra stopped to pray at a church during a visit to Stockholm, Sweden. Inside the church was a coffin containing a corpse. Mr. Sierra prayed for the dead man's soul for 20 minutes, and then he saw a book that asked people who had prayed for the man to sign their names and write their addresses. Mr. Sierra did so, and a few weeks later, people from Stockholm contacted him. The dead man was 73-year-old Jens Svenson, a millionaire with no close relatives. In his will, Mr. Svenson had written, "Whoever prays for my soul gets all my belongings." Mr. Sierra became a millionaire.

**A Jewish Boy and a Catholic Priest**

In Poland, during World War II, a Jewish mother gave her son to a Christian couple to take care of, saying that if anything happened to her and her husband, the couple should send the son to some relatives abroad. Eventually, the couple learned that the boy's parents had been killed, so they took the boy to a Catholic priest so that the boy could be baptized. However, the priest learned the story of the boy, and since the boy would be sent to Jewish relatives, he declined to baptize the boy out of respect for the boy's heritage and the sensitivities of his relatives. That priest was Cardinal Karol Wojtyla, who later became known by the name Pope John Paul II.

**Free Travel**

Mother Teresa and some members of her Missionaries of Charity flew all around the world, spending money on airplane tickets for necessary travel related to her charitable efforts. One day, she offered, half-jokingly, to serve as a stewardess on Air India in return for free airfare. Air India turned down Mother Teresa's offer to be a stewardess, but thereafter let her and the Missionaries of Charity fly free on all of its flights. This freed up money for the Missionaries of Charity to spend on helping poor people.

**The Lord's Prayer**

Sister Peggy Fannon, RN, worked in a burn unit for children at St. Joseph's Hospital, where she used both her nursing and religious training. For example, a boy who had been burned needed to enter a whirlpool bath, but the water stung his wounds—something very common for burn patients. To take his mind off the sting as he entered the whirlpool, she would suggest to him, "Let's say the Lord's Prayer together."

**"If You Can't Give Anything, Give a Pleasant Smile"**

Comedian Will Rogers was attending church one day when the minister spoke about the church debt and urged everyone to contribute generously so the debt could be paid off. As the collection plate was being passed around, the minister joked, "If you can't give anything, give a pleasant smile." When the collection plate reached Mr. Rogers, he didn't give any money, but instead grinned widely. The next morning, however, he sent a check to the minister. The check was big enough to pay off the entire debt owed by the church.

**"It is No Secret What God Can Do"**

Cordell Brown is a minister who has cerebral palsy and who ministers to people with handicaps. He started Camp Echoing Hills, a summer camp for handicapped adults, in Warsaw, Ohio, and he has established several residence facilities for handicapped adults throughout Ohio. While growing up, he often had a rough time at high school. Because of his cerebral palsy, trying to open his locker was quite an experience. One day, he was embarrassed when several classmates gathered around to watch him attempt to open his locker. Later, he began to fit in and even became manager of the football team. On the bus ride home after a game, after the obligatory rendition of "Ninety-Nine Bottles of Beer on the Wall," the team even sang a song in his honor. Because the team knew Mr. Brown was religious, the team sang "It is No Secret What God Can Do."

**"This Belongs to You as Well as Me"**

When he was an officer in the military, Saint Martin of Tours saw a beggar wearing rags in very cold weather. He had no money or food to give to the beggar, so he took his sword and cut his warm red-wool cloak in two and gave half to the beggar, saying, "We are brothers, my friend. This belongs to you as well as me."

# Chapter 15: WAR

**A Brave Canadian**

Robert Carson, the brother of environmentalist Rachel Carson, fought in World War I. In a letter home, he described a battle between two planes, one Canadian and the other German. The Germans shot away part of a wing of the Canadian plane, unbalancing it and making it wobble in the air. Fortunately, one of the two Canadians inside was able to crawl out on the wing of the plane and hang from its end, balancing the plane and allowing it to fly. The Germans could have easily shot the plane out of the sky, but they were impressed with the courage of the Canadian and let the plane land safely.

**After Pearl Harbor**

Before Pearl Harbor, Francis Aebi, whose ancestry is Swiss, and Tamaki Ninomiya, whose ancestry is Japanese, grew roses professionally in Contra Costa County in northern California. After Pearl Harbor, Mr. Ninomiya was sent to an American concentration camp for people—including U.S. citizens—of Japanese descent. While Mr. Ninomiya was in the concentration camp, Mr. Aebi took care of Mr. Ninomiya's land and business without pay. When Mr. Ninomiya was released from the concentration camp, he discovered that his land had been well taken care of, and Mr. Aebi presented him with a bankbook containing all the profits from the business.

**Becoming a Nurse's Aide**

In 1917, while World War I was raging, Amelia Earhart spent Christmas in Canada, where she learned that war results in very badly wounded soldiers. She wrote, "There for the first time I realized what world war meant. Instead of new uniforms and brass bands, I saw only the results of four years' desperate struggle: men without arms and legs, men who were paralyzed, and men who were blind. One day I saw four one-legged men at once, walking as best they could down the street together." The experience helped her decide to take nurses' training and become a nurse's aide in Toronto's Spadina Military Hospital.

**Water for an Enemy Soldier**

On 30 August 1862, the Union and Confederate forces battled at Richmond, Kentucky. After the battle, William Wilkerson of Fayette County,

Kentucky, witnessed a remarkable good deed performed for an enemy soldier. As Mr. Wilkerson searched for the corpse of a friend so he could give it to the friend's father, he saw two wounded soldiers: a Confederate soldier whose legs had been mangled by a cannonball, and a Union soldier who had been shot twice. With parched lips, the Union soldier was crying out for water. The Confederate soldier had water, and since the Union soldier was so badly wounded that he could not move, the Confederate soldier used his arms to drag himself to the Union soldier and give him water. The two soldiers then clasped each other's hands. The Confederate soldier died shortly afterward, and the Union soldier died the following day.

# Chapter 16: AIDS AND MEDICINE

**"But for Her, I'd Have Withered Away"**

In parts of Africa, children and elderly people can be seen but not people in the middle. Why not? AIDS has devastated those people. Of course, people react to AIDS in different ways. Henning Mankell, author of *I Die, But My Memory Lives On*, tells a story about two people named Gladys and Christine, both of them young mothers with HIV. Gladys reacted to HIV by sitting in a dark room and waiting to die. Christine, although she, like Gladys, did not make enough money to buy the medicine that might save or prolong her life, kept as active as possible. One day, Christine visited Gladys in her darkened room and talked to her. She kept on visiting and talking to her, and one day Gladys got up and started living life again instead of waiting to die. Christine had told her that both of them needed to be responsible for their children. She added that they had to live as long as possible to take care of their children and not wait for death, which would come someday on its own. Mr. Mankell asked Gladys what she would have done if Christine had not visited her and talked to her. Gladys replied, "I'd still have been sitting there, waiting to die. ... I feel infinitely grateful to Christine. But for her, I'd have withered away."

**"Nothing Out of the Ordinary"**

Danny, a single gay man from Northern Ireland, got the HIV virus, and he worried—rightly—about how other people would treat him. For example, his own brother would not let him near his children—the brother's wife was afraid that the children would get AIDS. Fortunately, other people knew that proper precautions prevent the transmission of the HIV virus. He told a friend whose family he was friendly with that he was HIV-positive, and the friend told his wife. The next morning, Danny saw the friend's wife and their son, Jim. He worried that she might walk—or run—away from him, but instead everything happened as it normally did. The friend's wife told their son, "Look who's here, Jim," as she normally did, and little Jim came running toward Danny, shouting, "Danny, Danny, hug," as he normally did. Danny gratefully says, "There was nothing out of the ordinary—just this woman being the same with me as she'd always been."

**Shaking Hands with AIDS**

In a London hospital in 1987, Diana, Princess of Wales, publicly shook hands with nine men who were dying of AIDS. This may not seem like much, but the extensive media coverage taught millions of people that you don't get AIDS from shaking hands and chatting with someone who has AIDS. Princess Di said, "You can shake hands with people with AIDS and give them a hug. Heavens knows, they need it."

**"This Woman is Dealing with AIDS"**

As part of the AIDS Resource Foundation for Children, Faye Zealand has much experience with people who have HIV or AIDS. At the funeral of a person who had died of AIDS, Ms. Zealand was crying. A woman who was HIV positive and whose daughter was HIV positive came up to her, hugged her, and comforted her. Ms. Zealand looked at the woman and thought, "This woman is dealing with AIDS. She is dealing with the fact that the child with her has AIDS. And here she is consoling me."

**"Let It Be as Free as the Air We Breathe"**

Polio used to be a major killer and crippler of children. Fortunately, Albert Sabin invented a vaccine that used live viruses to fight polio, saving the lives or preventing the paralysis of millions of children. (Earlier, Jonas Salk had invented a vaccine that used dead viruses.) Mr. Sabin refused to patent his vaccine; that way, it would reach many more children very much faster. Similarly, dentistry used to be painful before the discovery of anesthesia. Fortunately, the 19th-century dentist Dr. Horace Wells of Hartford, Connecticut discovered that nitrous oxide deadened the pain. When friends wanted him to patent his discovery, he replied, "No! Let it be as free as the air we breathe."

**Free Medical Care**

Prem Sharma, the co-founder of the first residential shelter in the United States for Asian-American women who are victims of domestic violence, was influenced by the good deeds of her father. When he was 75 years old, he passed his exams in homeopathy and started using his knowledge to help other people. He treated all of his patients free of charge.

**Letting a Soul Fly Free**

Navy nurse Steven H. Brant once cared for a dying Native American who worried that his soul would not be able to rise to the afterlife unless he died in the open air. As you would expect, dying in an air-conditioned hospital with the windows shut tight terrified him. However, as the Native American was taking his last few breaths, Mr. Brant and some other nurses quickly pushed his wheeled bed down the hallway and outside in the open air. Mr. Brant says about the Native American, "He died in peace, knowing that his spirit would be released."

# Chapter 17: POLITICS

**"I Fine You $10 for Stealing"**

Fiorello La Guardia served as a night-court judge during the Depression. One night, a woman appeared before him who was guilty of stealing food so she could feed her hungry children. Mr. La Guardia heard the case, and then he ruled: "I fine you $10 for stealing, and I fine everyone else in this courtroom, myself included, 50 cents for living in a city where a woman is forced to steal to feed her children." The money collected in the courtroom was used to pay the woman's fine, and the leftover money was given to her.

**"Tell Me about Habitat"**

Former United States President Jimmy Carter volunteered for Habitat for Humanity, where he helped build low-cost housing for people who could not otherwise afford it. He even started the Jimmy Carter Work Project for Habitat for Humanity. Each year, President and Mrs. Carter and thousands of volunteers spent a week at a particular work site building housing. In Philadelphia, they built a 10-unit rowhouse; in Chicago, they built a 4-unit townhouse; and in New York City, they built a 6-story, 19-unit building. He said, "I get a lot more recognition for building houses in partnership with people than I ever got for the Camp David Accord or for Salt II, or for all our projects in Africa and Asia or anything I do now since I left the White House. I can walk down the aisles of airplanes talking with people, and invariably the number one thing that everybody says is, 'Tell me about Habitat.'"

**A Friend in Deed**

During the Civil War, lots of people wrote President Abraham Lincoln to ask for pardons. Usually, their letters were accompanied with statements of support from influential people. One day, a letter arrived that asked for a pardon but had no accompanying statements of support from influential people. President Lincoln asked, "Has this man no friends?" Hearing that the man in fact lacked friends, President Lincoln said, "Then I will be his friend"—and he signed the pardon.

**Surveyor Abraham Lincoln**

As a surveyor, Abraham Lincoln platted Petersburg, Illinois. Years later, a dispute arose in the law courts regarding the location of a property line. An old Irishman who had known Mr. Lincoln was able to pinpoint the source of the problem. When Mr. Lincoln was surveying the town, he had seen that a proposed street would cut off three or four feet of a fellow's house. He then said, "It's all he's got in the world and he could never get another. I reckon it won't hurt anything if I skew the line a little and miss him."

**Unneeded Gifts of Money**

In the first half of the 20th century, Texas journalist/historian Don Hampton Biggers was a friend of Senator Tom Connally. Each year, Senator Connally used to send Mr. Biggers a Stetson hat as a birthday present. Later, Senator Connally was under the impression that his friend was in financial distress, so he began to send gifts of money. Mr. Biggers was not in financial distress, so he found a charitable way to use the money after matching the amount of each gift. (If Senator Connally sent him $25—a lot of money back then—Mr. Biggers added $25 of his own money to it.) Once he bought clothing for the children of a needy family; another time he paid the hospital bill of a destitute family.

**Defending the Unpopular**

On 5 March 1770, during a tense time in relations between Great Britain and its American colonies, British soldiers fired shots into a hostile crowd. Three American colonists fell dead immediately; two others lay mortally wounded. This became known as the Boston Massacre. As you would expect, the British soldiers who fired on the American colonists were widely hated. As you might not expect, they were put on trial for murder. Because the British soldiers were so widely hated, they found it difficult to get a lawyer to represent them. Fortunately, John Adams, a well-known lawyer (and later the second President of the United States), believed that all people are entitled to competent legal representation, and he defended the British soldiers so ably that they were found innocent and released from prison.

**Comforting a Hero**

In 1961, John Seigenthaler tried to help some Nashville, Tennessee, college students who were being attacked in Montgomery, Alabama, because they were "Freedom Riders" who traveled through the South to register black voters. The thugs also attacked him and left him unconscious. He was taken to a hospital in Montgomery, where he was soon visited by Will D. Campbell, who told him, "I come representing 40 million Protestants, and one of those bastards hit you in the head last night." With Mr. Campbell was Nashville attorney George Barrett, who told him, "On behalf of 150 million Catholics, I bring you greetings."

**Winning Civil Rights**

Mohandas (Mahatma) Gandhi worked as a lawyer in South Africa. Unfortunately, because of his Indian heritage, he was regarded as "colored," and like the other Indians in South Africa, he was not permitted to cross provincial borders. He responded with nonviolent protest, organizing Indians to cross provincial borders in mass groups of people. The first mass group of Indians crossed the border, were arrested and thrown in prison, and the second mass group of Indians crossed the border, were arrested and thrown in prison, and so on. Quickly, the South Africans realized that their prisons could not hold 20,000 Indians, and so the Indians won civil rights. Later, Martin Luther King, Jr., used similar tactics to win civil rights for African Americans in the United States.

# Chapter 18: MISCELLANEOUS

**Spoiling Minimum-Wage "Girls"**

When architect Julia Morgan was designing a YWCA to be built in San Francisco, she told the board of directors that in one area of the YWCA was some extra space, so she had designed a couple of private dining areas with small kitchens so that the residents could cook a meal, invite a few friends over, and entertain them. One of the directors said, "These are minimum-wage girls there. Why spoil them?" Ms. Morgan replied, "That's just the reason."

**Falling Through the Ice**

Robert Fulton, who showed that steamboats could be a profitable mode of transportation, and his lawyer, Thomas Addis Emmet, traveled together during the winter of 1815. To cross the Hudson River, they walked on the ice of the river to a small boat that would carry them the rest of the way across. The ice Mr. Emmet was walking on broke, and he fell through the ice into the cold water. Mr. Fulton managed to pull him out, but in saving the life of his lawyer, he got soaked and fell ill from being exposed to the cold. On 23 February 1815, Mr. Fulton died in New York City at the age of 49.

**A Personal Library**

In the 1850s in Allegheny, Pennsylvania, a wealthy old man named Colonel James Anderson owned a personal library containing 400 books. Because Allegheny (which is now part of Pittsburgh) did not have a public library, each Saturday Colonel Anderson allowed working-class boys into his home to read the books. He also allowed them to borrow books. One of the boys reading his books was Andrew Carnegie, who became a wealthy industrialist and helped fund 2,811 free public libraries before dying in 1919.

**"Breezing" Her Along**

Nancy "Kati" Garner became the first woman to graduate from the United States Navy Diving School, SCUBA, in 1973. This school is definitely physically and mentally rigorous, and most people don't make it. Although she was the first woman to graduate, she discovered that the men she was training with wanted her to graduate from the school. At one point in the school, the trainees were required to jog faster than Ms. Garner was used to, so the men helped her get through the jogging. Ms. Garner says, "They would help me out by putting their arms around me and breeze me along."

### Candy From a Child's Ears

Magician Herrmann the Great was kind to children. While walking down a street, he would frequently pause to perform the trick of pulling candy from a child's ears and then present the child with the candy.

### Watkuweis

When the Lewis and Clark expedition encountered the Native Americans known as the Nez Percé, Meriwether Lewis, William Clark, and their men were tired and hungry. The Nez Percé debated what they should do with the white men, and most thought that they should kill them and take their property. However, a Nez Percé woman named Watkuweis (her name means "Returned from a Far Country") spoke up for the white explorers. Earlier, she had been kidnapped by another tribe and sold to some white people who had treated her well, and she argued to Nez Percé chief Twisted Hair that the kindness that white people had shown to her earlier should be returned to these white explorers now. If not for her, the Lewis and Clark expedition would have ended disastrously.

### Bringing Good Out of Evil

In 1932, a great tragedy happened to the family of Charles and Anne Morrow Lindbergh—their 20-month-old son, Charles, Jr., was kidnapped and murdered, although the Lindberghs paid the $50,000 ransom demanded for his safe return. Because of the tragedy, they no longer wished to live in their home near Hopewell, New Jersey, so they brought good out of evil by donating their home to New Jersey so it could be used as a residence for homeless children.

### Despising Charity

Lillian D. Wald was a major figure in establishing public-health nursing in the United States. In New York's Lower East Side, she and other nurses provided home nursing in the late 1800s and the early 1900s. Because the people she served despised charity, she and the other nurses charged 10 cents per visit, but if a family could not pay they would not press for payment.

### True Charity—Touching the Poor

Many people are willing to donate money to the poor, but they are unwilling to do more than that, although sometimes what they don't do would be more appreciated than what they actually do. For example, a man saw a beggar on the street, and taking pity, he stopped and searched his pockets for money to give to the beggar. Finding nothing to put in the beggar's outstretched hand, he grasped the beggar's hand and shook it, saying, "I am sorry, my friend, but I have no money to give you." The beggar replied, "You have no need to apologize. I thank you for this handshake, for it, my friend, is true charity."

# CONCLUSION

**Trying to Be Better Than We Really Are**

In 1946, when Avi, children's book author of *Windcatcher*, was a child, he loved comic books. He was also aware that wounded veterans of World War II loved comic books. Therefore, he decided to emulate some of his comic-book heroes who displayed the characteristic of selflessness by holding a comic-book drive for the wounded veterans. He spoke passionately at classes at his school, and a veritable cornucopia of comic books poured in. Unfortunately, once young Avi had the comic books that had been donated to the wounded vets, he found it hard to hand them over to a veterans hospital because he hadn't read them yet. Therefore, he went on a comic-book reading spree, reading them all the time he could. When his mother asked if he was ready to send them to the wounded veterans, he replied, "I haven't finished reading them all." She asked, "Who are they are for?" Unfortunately, young Avi was too busy reading comic books to answer. Eventually, his mother sent the comic books to a veterans hospital while young Avi was at school. Young Avi then realized that he had been selfish and was therefore not suited to be a comic-book hero. However, he did receive a wonderful letter that told him, "America is great because of unselfish patriots like you." (Sometimes, we try to be better than we really are; although such efforts may result in failure, they ought to be applauded.)

# BIBLIOGRAPHY


Aaseng, Nathan. *Football's Cunning Coaches*. Minneapolis, MN: Lerner Publications Company, 1981.

Adams, Franklin P., et. al. *Percy Hammond: A Symposium in Tribute*. Garden City, NY: Doubleday, Doran & Co., Inc., 1936.

Adler, Bill. *Baseball Wit*. New York: Crown Publishers, Inc., 1986.

Acker, Kerry. *Nina Simone*. Philadelphia, PA: Chelsea House Publishers, 2004.

Alda, Frances. *Men, Women, and Tenors*. Boston, MA: Houghton Mifflin Company, 1937.

Algeranoff, H. *My Years With Pavlova*. London: William Heinemann, Ltd., 1957.

Allen, Everett S. *Famous American Humorous Poets*. New York: Dodd, Mead & Company, 1968.

Allen, Steve. *More Funny People*. New York: Stein and Day, Publishers, 1982.

Arden, Eve. *Three Phases of Eve: An Autobiography*. New York: St. Martin's Press, 1985.

Auerbach, Arnold M. *Funny Men Don't Laugh*. Garden City, NY: Doubleday and Co., Inc., 1965.

Benson, Constance. *Mainly Players: Bensonian Memories*. London: Thornton Butterworth, Ltd., 1926.

Berenstain, Stan and Jan. *Down a Sunny Dirt Road: An Autobiography*. New York: Random House, 2002.

Berger, Phil. *The Last Laugh: The World of the Stand-Up Comics*. New York: William Morris and Co., Inc., 1975.

Bessette, Roland L. *Mario Lanza: Tenor in Exile*. Portland, OR: Amadeus Press, 1999.

Biggers, Don Hampton. *Buffalo Guns & Barbed Wire*. Lubbock, TX: Texas Tech University Press, 1991.

Billings, Henry and Melissa. *Eccentrics: 21 Stories of Unusual and Remarkable People*. Providence, RI: Jamestown Publishers, 1987.

Bing, Sir Rudolf. *A Knight at the Opera*. New York: G.P. Putnam's Sons, 1981.

Biracree, Tom. *Althea Gibson: Tennis Champion*. New York: Chelsea House Publishers, 1989.

Block, Gay, and Malka Drucker. *Rescuers: Portraits of Moral Courage in the Holocaust*. New York: Holmes and Meier Publishers, Inc., 1992.

Blumberg, Arthur, and Phyllis Blumberg. *The Unwritten Curriculum: Things Learned But Not Taught in Schools*. Thousand Oaks, CA: Corwin Press, Inc., 1994.

Bolden, Tonya. *Wake Up Our Souls: A Celebration of Black American Artists*. New York: Harry N. Abrams, Inc., 2004.

Borns, Betsy. *Comic Lives: Inside the World of American Stand-Up Comedy*. New York: Simon and Schuster, Inc., 1987.

Bourke, Dale Hanson. *Everyday Miracles: Holy Moments in a Mother's Day*. Dallas, TX: Word Publishing, 1989.

Boxer, Tim. *The Jewish Celebrity Hall of Fame*. New York: Shapolsky Publishers, 1987.

Bredeson, Carmen, and Ralph Thibodeau. *Ten Great American Composers*. Berkeley Heights, NJ: Enslow Publishers, Inc., 2002.

Brennan, Christine. *Inside Edge: A Revealing Journey into the Secret World of Figure Skating*. New York: Scribner, 1996.

Brown, Cordell. *I am What I am by the Grace of God*. Warsaw, OH: Echoing Hills Village Foundation, 1996.

Brown, Joe E. *Laughter is a Wonderful Thing*. As told to Ralph Hancock. New York: A. S. Barnes and Co., 1956.

Bryan III, J. *Merry Gentlemen (and One Lady)*. New York: Atheneum, 1985.

Burns, George. *All My Best Friends*. Written with David Fisher. New York: Putnam Publishing Group, 1989.

Burns, George. *Gracie: A Love Story*. New York: G.P. Putnam's Sons, 1988.

Cabot, Meg. *Perfect Princess*. New York: HarperCollins Publishers, 2004.

Campbell, Archie. *Archie Campbell: An Autobiography*. With Ben Bryd. Memphis, TN: Memphis State University Press, 1981.

Cantor, Eddie. *As I Remember Them*. New York: Duell, Sloan and Pearce, 1963. (Mr. Cantor's collaborator for most of these pieces was Vivian M. Bowes, to whom he gives credit on the acknowledgements page.)

Cantor, Eddie. *Take My Life*. Written with Jane Kesner Ardmore. Garden City, NY: Doubleday, 1957.

Caplin, Elliott. *Al Capp Remembered*. Bowling Green, OH: Bowling Green State University Popular Press, 1994.

Cardus, Neville, editor. *Kathleen Ferrier: A Memoir*. London: Hamish Hamilton, Ltd., 1954.

Cartwright, Nancy. *My Life as a 10-Year-Old Boy*. New York: Hyperion, 2000.

Caruso, Dorothy. *Enrico Caruso: His Life and Death*. New York: Simon and Schuster, Inc., 1945.

Certner, Simon, editor. *101 Jewish Stories for Schools, Clubs and Camps*. New York: Jewish Education Committee Press, 1961.

Chadwick, Roxane. *Anne Morrow Lindbergh: Pilot and Poet*. Minneapolis, MN: Lerner Publications Company, 1987.

Chaliapine, Feodor Ivanovitch. *Pages From My Life: An Autobiography*. Translated by H.M. Buck. New York and London: Harper and Brothers, Publishers, 1927.

Chippendale, Lisa A. *Yo-Yo Ma: A Cello Superstar Brings Music to the World*. Berkeley Heights, NJ: Enslow Publishers, Inc., 1994.

Chotzinoff, Samuel. *Toscanini: An Intimate Portrait*. New York: Alfred A. Knopf, 1956.

Clower, Jerry. *Life Everlaughter: The Heart and Humor of Jerry Clower*. Nashville, TN: Rutledge Hill Press, 1987.

Clower, Jerry. *Stories From Home*. Jackson, MS: University Press of Mississippi, 1992.

Cohen, Joel. *Odd Moments in Baseball*. New York: Scholastic, Inc., 2000.

Cohen, Sasha. *Fire on Ice: Autobiography of a Champion Figure Skater*. With Amanda Maciel. New York: HarperCollins Publishers, 2005.

Coombs, Karen Mueller. *Jackie Robinson: Baseball's Civil Rights Legend*. Springfield, NJ: Enslow Publications, Inc., 1997.

Crum, Jimmy, and Carole Gerber. *How About That! Jimmy Crum: Fifty Years of Cliffhangers and Barn-Burners*. Columbus, OH: Fine Line Graphics, 1993.

Crutcher, Chris. *King of the Mild Frontier*. New York: Greenwillow Books, 2003.

Cruz, Barbara C. *Rubén Blades: Salsa Singer and Social Activist*. Springfield, NJ: Enslow Publications, Inc., 1997.

Cytron, Barry D. *Fire! The Library is Burning*. Minneapolis, MN: Lerner Publications Company, 1988.

DeBartolo, Dick. *Good Days and MAD*. New York: Thunder's Mouth Press, 1994.

dePaola, Tomie. *What a Year*. New York: G.P. Putnam's Sons, 2002.

DeVos, Dick. *Rediscovering American Values: The Foundations of Our Freedom in the 21st Century*. New York: The Penguin Group, 1997.

Dole, Bob. *Great Presidential Wit*. New York: Scribner, 2001.

Dolin, Anton. *Alicia Markova: Her Life and Art*. New York: Hermitage House, 1953.

Dommermuth-Costa, Carol. *Emily Dickinson: Singular Poet*. Minneapolis, MN: Lerner Publications Company, 1998.

Doonan, Simon. *Confessions of a Window Dresser*. New York: Penguin Studio, 1998.

Dosick, Wayne. *Golden Rules: The Ten Ethical Rules Parents Need to Teach Their Children*. San Francisco. CA: HarperSanFrancisco, 1995.

Edwards, Judith. *Lewis and Clark's Journey of Discovery in American History*. Springfield, NJ: Enslow Publications, Inc., 1999.

Epstein, Lawrence J. *A Treasury of Jewish Inspirational Stories*. Northvale, NJ: Jason Aronson, Inc., 1993.

Erskine, Carl. *Carl Erskine's Tales from the Dodger Dugout*. Champaigne, IL: Sports Publishing Inc., 2000.

Farrell, Suzanne. *Holding On to the Air*. New York: Summit Books, 1990.

Feather, Leonard, and Jack Tracy. *Laughter from the Hip: The Lighter Side of Jazz*. New York: Da Capo Press, Inc., 1979.

Flammang, James M. *Robert Fulton: Inventor and Steamboat Builder*. Berkeley Heights, NJ: Enslow Publications, Inc., 1999.

Ford, Carin T. *Jackie Robinson: "All I Ask is That You Respect Me as a Human Being."* Berkeley Heights, NJ: Enslow Publishers, Inc., 2005.

Ford, Michael Thomas. *The Voices of AIDS: Twelve Unforgettable People Talk About How AIDS has Changed Their Lives*. New York: Morrow Junior Books, 1995.

Forkos, Heather. *Dorothy "Dot" Richardson*. Philadelphia, PA: Chelsea House Publishers, 2001.

Gaines, Ann Graham. *American Photographers: Capturing the Image*. Berkeley Heights, NJ: Enslow Publishers, Inc., 2002.

Gaines, Ann. *Coco Chanel*. Philadelphia, PA: Chelsea House Publishers, 2004.

Garagiola, Joe. *It's Anybody's Ballgame*. New York: Jove Books, 1988.

Garden, Mary, and Louis Biancolli. *Mary Garden's Story*. New York: Simon and Schuster, Inc., 1951.

Gaster, Moses. *The Exempla of the Rabbis: Being a Collection of Exempla, Apologues and Tales Culled from Hebrew Manuscripts and Rare Hebrew Books*. New York: Ktav Publishing House, Inc., 1968.

Giles, Sarah. *Fred Astaire: His Friends Talk*. New York: Doubleday, 1988.

Glatzer, Nahum N., editor. *Hammer on the Rock: A Short Midrash Reader*. Translated by Jacob Sloan. New York: Schocken Books, 1962.

Glenn, Menahem G. *Israel Salanter: Religious-Ethical Thinker*. New York: Bloch Publishing Company, 1953.

Goh, Chan Hon. *Beyond the Dance: A Ballerina's Life*. With Cary Fagan. Toronto, Ontario, Canada: Tundra Books, 2002.

Goldenstern, Joyce. *American Women Against Violence*. Springfield, NJ: Enslow Publications, Inc., 1998.

Gordeeva, Ekaterina. *My Sergei: A Love Story*. With E.M. Swift. New York: Warner Books, Inc., 1996.

Gray, Hector. *An Actor Looks Back*. Hobart Tasmania: Cat and Fiddle Press, 1973.

Green, Joey. *Hi Bob! The Unofficial Guide to* The Bob Newhart Show. New York: St. Martin's Griffin, 1996. Advance uncorrected proofs.

Greenberg, Jan, and Sandra Jordan. *Andy Warhol: Prince of Pop*. New York: Delacorte Press, 2004.

Gregory, Dick. *Nigger: An Autobiography*. With Robert Lipsyte. New York: Dutton, 1964.

Gutman, Bill. *More Modern Women Superstars*. New York: Dodd, Mead and Company, 1979.

Gutman, Bill. *Shooting Stars: The Women of Pro Basketball*. New York: Randam House, 1998.

Hacker, Carlotta. *Humanitarians*. New York: Crabtree Publishing Company, 1999.

Hajdusiewicz, Babs Bell. *Mary Carter Smith: African-American Storyteller*. Springfield, NJ: Enslow Publications, Inc., 1995.

Hamill, Dorothy. *On and Off the Ice*. With Elva Clairmont. New York: Alfred A. Knopf, Inc. 1983.

Haney, Lynn. *Ride 'em, Cowgirl!* New York: G.P. Putnam's Sons, 1975.

Haskins, James. *Babe Ruth and Hank Aaron: The Home Run Kings*. New York: Lothrop, Lee & Shepard Company, 1974.

Haskins, Jim, and N.R. Mitgang. *Mr. Bojangles: The Story of Bill Robinson*. New York: William Morrow and Company, Inc., 1988.

Hauser, Hillary. *Scuba Diving*. New York: Harvey House, Publishers, 1976.

Henry, Linda Gambee, and James Douglas Henry. *The Soul of the Caring Nurse: Stories and Resources for Revitalizing Professional Passion*. Washington, D.C.: American Nurses Association, 2004.

Heylbut, Rose, and Aimé Gerber. *Backstage at the Opera*. New York: Thomas Y. Crowell Company, 1937.

Herda, D. J. *Thurgood Marshall: Civil Rights Champion*. Springfield, NJ: Enslow Publications, Inc., 1995.

Himelstein, Shmuel. *A Touch of Wisdom, A Touch of Wit*. Brooklyn, NY: Mesorah Publications, Limited, 1991.

Hoffman, Richard. *Some Musical Recollections of Fifty Years*. New York: Charles Scribner's Sons, 1910.

Hollingsworth, Amy. *The Simple Faith of Mister Rogers*. Nashville, TN: Integrity Publishers, 2005.

Hudry, Francois. *Hugues Cuenod: With a Nimble Voice*. Trans. Albert Fuller. Hillsdale, NY: Pendragon Press, 1998.

Humphrey, Laning, compiler. *The Humor of Music and Other Oddities in the Art*. Boston, MA: Crescendo Publishing Company, 1971.

Jacobsen, Peter. *Embedded Balls*. With Jack Sheehan. New York: G.P. Putnam's Sons, 2005.

Jewell, Geri. *Geri*. With Stewart Weiner. New York: William Morrow and Co., Inc., 1984.

Karolyi, Bela, and Nancy Ann Richardson. *Feel No Fear: The Power, Passion, and Politics of a Life in Gymnastics*. New York: Hyperion, 1994.

Kistler, Darci. *Ballerina: My Story*. With Alicia Kistler. New York: Pocket Books, Inc., 1993.

Karkar, Jack, and Waltraud Karkar, compilers and editors. *... And They Danced On*. Wausau, WI: Aardvark Enterprises, 1989.

Katella-Cofrancesco, Kathy. *Economic Causes*. Brookfield, CT: Twenty-First Century Books, 1998.

Kaufmann, Helen L. *Anecdotes of Music and Musicians*. New York: Grosset & Dunlap, Publishers, 1960.

Kent, Zachary. *Andrew Carnegie: Steel King and Friends to Libraries*. Berkeley Heights, NJ: Enslow Publications, Inc., 1999.

Kertzer, Morris N. *Tell Me, Rabbi*. New York: Bloch Publishing Company, 1976.

Kindred, Dave. *Heroes, Fools, and Other Dreamers: A Sportswriter's Gallery of Extraordinary People*. Atlanta, GA: Longstreet Press, 1988.

Kinney, Jack. *Walt Disney and Other Assorted Characters: An Unauthorized Account of the Early Years at Disney's*. New York: Harmony Books, 1988.

Knapp, Ron. *American Legends of Rock*. Springfield, NJ: Enslow Publications, Inc., 1996.

Kornfield, Jack, and Christina Feldman. *Soul Food: Stories to Nourish the Spirit and the Heart*. San Francisco, CA: HarperSanFrancisco, 1996. This is a revised edition of their book *Stories of the Spirit, Stories of the Heart* (1991).

Ladré, Illaria Obidenna. *Illaria Obidenna Ladré: Memoirs of a Child of Theatre Street*. With Nancy Whyte. Seattle, WA: The Author, 1988.

Lahee, Henry C. *Famous Singers of To-day and Yesterday*. Boston, MA: L. C. Page and Company, 1898.

Lawton, Mary. *Schumann-Heink: The Last of the Titans*. New York: The Macmillan Company, 1928.

Lazo, Caroline. *Alice Walker: Freedom Writer*. Minneapolis, MN: Lerner Publications Company, 2000.

Leipold, L. Edmond. *Famous American Artists*. Minneapolis, MN: T. S. Denison and Company, Inc., 1969.

Leno, Jay. *Leading With My Chin*. With Bill Zehme. New York: HarperCollins Publishers, Inc., 1996.

Leonard, Sheldon. *And the Show Goes On: Broadway and Hollywood Adventures*. New York: Limelight, 1994.

Lewis, Gregg, and Deborah Shaw Lewis. *Today's Heroes: Joni Eareckson Tada*. Grand Rapids, MI: Zonderkidz, 2002.

Lewis, Mildred, and Milton Lewis. *Famous Modern Newspaper Writers*. New York: Dodd, Mead & Company, 1962.

Lilley, Stephen R. *Fighters Against American Slavery*. San Diego, CA: Lucent Books, 1999.

Lisandrelli, Elaine Slivinski. *Maya Angelou: More Than a Poet*. Berkeley Heights, NJ: Enslow Publications, Inc., 1996.

Long, Rod. *Belly Laughs*. Renton, WI: Talion Publishing, 1999.

Lowry, Lois. *Number the Stars*. New York: Bantam Doubleday Dell Books for Young Readers, 1989.

Lyman, Darryl. *Holocaust Rescuers: Ten Stories of Courage*. Springfield, NJ: Enslow Publications, Inc., 1999.

Macnow, Glen. *Sports Great Charles Barkley*. Hillside, NJ: Enslow Publications, Inc., 1992.

Malone, Mary. *Will Rogers: Cowboy Philosopher*. Springfield, NJ: Enslow Publications, Inc., 1996.

Mandelbaum, Yitta Halberstam. *Holy Brother: Inspiring Stories and Enchanted Tales About Rabbi Shlomo Carlebach*. Northvale, NJ: Jason Aronson Inc., 1997.

Mankell, Henning. *I Die, But My Memory Lives On*. New York: The New Press, 2004.

Marcus, Leonard S., compiler and editor. *Author Talk*. New York: Simon and Schuster Books for Young Readers, 2000.

Maverick, Jr., Maury. *Texas Iconoclast*. Edited by Allan O. Kownslar. Fort Worth, TX: Texas Christian University Press, 1997.

Maybarduk, Linda. *The Dancer Who Flew: A Memoir of Rudolf Nureyev*. Toronto, Ontario, Canada: Tundra Books, 1999.

McArthur, Debra. *Raoul Wallenberg: Rescuing Thousands from the Nazis' Grasp*. Berkeley Heights, NJ: Enslow Publishers, Inc., 2005.

McArthur, Edwin. *Flagstad: A Personal Memoir*. New York: Alfred A. Knopf, 1965.

McNeil, Legs, and Gillian McCain, editors. *Please Kill Me: The Uncensored Oral History of Punk*. New York: Penguin Books, 1997.

Miller, John. *Ralph Richardson: The Authorized Biography*. London: Sidgwick and Jackson, 1995.

Miller, Norma. *Swinging' at the Savoy*. With Evette Jensen. Philadelphia, PA: Temple University Press, 1996.

Mingo, Jack. *The Juicy Parts*. New York: The Berkley Publishing Group, 1996.

Moore, Grace. *You're Only Human Once*. Garden City, NY: Doubleday, Doran and Co., Inc., 1944.

Morgan, Henry. *Here's Morgan!* New York: Barricade Books, Inc., 1994.

Mott, Robert L. *Radio Live! Television Live!: Those Golden Days When Horses Were Coconuts*. Jefferson, NC: McFarland & Company, Inc., Publishers, 2000.

Munch, Charles. *I am a Conductor*. New York: Oxford University Press, 1955.

Nachman, Gerald. *Seriously Funny: The Rebel Comedians of the 1950s and 1960s*. New York: Pantheon Books, 2003.

Neches, Solomon Michael. *Humorous Tales of Latter Day Rabbis*. New York: George Dobsevage, 1938.

Netzach, editor. *Chesed: The World is Built upon Kindness*. Edited and published by Netzach, a project of Mercaz HaTorah of California. North Hollywood, CA: Netzach, 1985.

Old, Wendie C. *Louis Armstrong: King of Jazz*. Springfield, NJ: Enslow Publications, Inc., 1998.

Oliner, Samuel P. *Do Unto Others: Extraordinary Acts of Ordinary People*. Cambridge, MA: Westview Press, 2003.

Olsen, Marilyn. *Women Who Risk: Profiles of Women in Extreme Sports*. New York: Hatherleigh Press, 2001.

Osborne, Angela. *Abigail Adams: Women's Rights Advocate*. New York: Chelsea House Publishers, 1989.

Parsons, Larry A. *A Funny Thing Happened on the Way to the School Library*. Englewood, CO: Libraries Unlimited, Inc., 1990.

Pearson, Hesketh. *Lives of the Wits*. New York: Harper & Row, Publishers, 1962.

Perrine, Laurence. *Literature: Structure, Sound, and Sense*. 2nd ed. New York: Harcourt Brace Jovanovich, Inc., 1974.

Pochocki, Ethel. *One-of-a-Kind Friends: Saints and Heroes for Kids*. Cincinnati, OH: St. Anthony Messenger Press, 1994.

Poley, Irvin C., and Ruth Verlenden Poley. *Friendly Anecdotes*. New York: Harper & Brothers, Publishers, 1950.

Pratt, Paula Bryant. *Martha Graham*. San Diego, CA: Lucent Books, 1995.

Presnall, Judith Janda. *Rachel Carson*. San Diego, CA: Lucent Books, 1995.

Procter-Gregg, Humphrey. *Beecham Remembered*. London: Gerald Duckworth & Company, Limited, 1976.

Rabinowicz, Rabbi Dr. H. *A Guide to Hassidism*. New York: Thomas Yoseloff, 1960.

Radner, Gilda. *It's Always Something*. New York: Avon Books, 1989.

Rayner, William P. *Wise Women*. New York: St. Martin's Press, 1983.

Reps, Paul, compiler. *Zen Flesh, Zen Bones*. Rutland, VT: Charles E. Tuttle Co., 1957.

Reynolds, Moira Davison. *Women Champions of Human Rights*. Jefferson, NC: McFarland and Company, Inc., 1991.

Richardson, Ann, and Dietmar Bolle, editors. *Wise Before Their Time: People with AIDS and HIV Talk About Their Lives*. London: Fount, 1992.

Rockwell, Bart. *World's Strangest Baseball Stories*. Mahwah, NJ: Watermill Press, 1993.

Rogers, Fred. *The World According to Mister Rogers*. New York: Hyperion, 2003.

Rolph, Daniel N. *My Brother's Keeper: Union and Confederate Soldiers' Acts of Mercy during the Civil War*. Mechanicsburg, PA: Stackpole Books, 2002.

Rossi, Alfred. *Astonish Us in the Morning: Tyrone Guthrie Remembered*. London: Hutchinson & Co., Publishers, 1977.

Russell, Fred, teller. *Funny Thing About Sports*. Nashville, TN: The McQuiddy Press, 1948.

Russell, Fred. *I'll Try Anything Twice*. Nashville, TN: The McQuiddy Press, 1945.

Ruth, Amy. *Mother Teresa*. Minneapolis, MN: Lerner Publications Company, 1999.

Salzberg, Sharon. *A Heart as Wide as the World: Stories on the Path to Lovingkindness*. Boston, MA: Shambhala Publications, Inc., 1997.

Samra, Cal and Rose Samra, editors. *Holy Hilarity*. Colorado Springs, CO: WaterBrook Press, 1999.

Samra, Cal, and Rose Samra, editors. *Holy Humor*. Colorado Springs, CO: WaterBrook Press, 1997.

Sanford, Herb. *Ladies and Gentlemen, The Garry Moore Show: Behind the Scenes When TV was New*. New York: Stein and Day, Publishers, 1976.

Savage, Jeff. *Top 10 Sports Bloopers and Who Made Them*. Berkeley Heights, NJ: Enslow Publications, Inc., 2000.

Scieszka, Jon, editor. *Guys Write for Guys Read*. New York: Viking, 2005.

Sessions, William H., collector. *Laughter in Quaker Grey*. York, England: William Sessions, Limited, 1966.

Sessions, William H., collector. *More Quaker Laughter*. York, England: William Sessions, Limited, 1974.

Shore, Nancy. *Amelia Earhart*. New York: Chelsea House Publishers, 1987.

Slezak, Walter. *What Time's the Next Swan?* Garden City, NY: Doubleday and Co., Inc., 1962.

Smith, H. Allen. *To Hell in a Handbasket*. Garden City, NY: Doubleday & Company, Inc., 1962.

Snead, Sam. *The Game I Love: Wisdom, Insight, and Instruction from Golf's Greatest Player*. With Fran Pirozzolo. New York: Ballantine Books, 1997.

Sorel, Nancy Caldwell, and Edward Sorel. *First Encounters: A Book of Memorable Meetings*. New York: Alfred A. Knopf, 1994.

Stier, Theodore. *With Pavlova Around the World*. London: Hurst & Blackett, Ltd., 1927.

Suponev, Michael. *Olga Korbut: A Biographical Portrait*. Garden City, NY: Doubleday and Company, Inc., 1975.

Szilard, Paul. *Under My Wings: My Life as an Impresario*. New York: Limelight Editions, 2002.

Taylor, Robert Lewis. *W.C. Fields: His Follies and Fortunes*. Garden City, NY: Doubleday and Company, Inc., 1949.

Telushkin, Rabbi Joseph. *Jewish Humor: What the Best Jewish Jokes Say About the Jews*. New York: William Morrow and Company, 1992.

Telushkin, Rabbi Joseph. *Jewish Wisdom: Ethical, Spiritual, and Historical Lessons from the Great Works and Thinkers*. New York: William Morrow and Company, Inc., 1994.

Torvill, Jayne, and Christopher Dean. *Torvill and Dean: The Autobiography of Ice Dancing's Greatest Stars*. With John Man. Secaucus, NJ: Carol Publishing Group, 1996.

Towle, Mike. *I Remember Arthur Ashe*. Nashville, TN: Cumberland House, 2001.

Tracy, Kathleen. *The Girl's Got Bite*. New York: St. Martin's Press, 2003.

Traubel, Helen. *St. Louis Woman*. New York: Duell, Sloan and Pearce, 1959.

True, Cynthia. *American Scream: The Bill Hicks Story*. New York: HarperEntertainment, 2002.

Tully, Jim. *A Dozen and One*. Hollywood, CA: Murray & Gee, Inc., Publishers, 1943.

Uecker, Bob, and Mickey Herskowitz. *Catcher in the Wry*. New York: G.P. Putnam's Sons, 1982.

Underwood, Peter. *Danny La Rue: Life's a Drag!* London: W. H. Allen & Co., Ltd., 1974.

Voskressenski, Alexei D., compiler and editor. *Cranks, Knaves, and Jokers of the Celestial*. Translated from the Chinese by Alexei Voskressenski and Vladimir Larin. Commack, NY: Nova Science Publishers, Inc., 1997.

Wade, Don. *"And Then Arnie Told Chi Chi ...."* Chicago, IL: Contemporary Books, 1993.

Wade, Mary Dodson. *Joan Lowery Nixon: Masterful Mystery Writer*. Berkeley Heights, NJ: Enslow Publishers, Inc., 2004.

Wadsworth, Ginger. *Julia Morgan: Architect of Dreams*. Minneapolis, MN: Lerner Publications Company, 1990.

Wagenknecht, Edward. *Seven Daughters of the Theater*. Norman, OK: University of Oklahoma Press, 1964.

Woog, Adam. *Magicians and Illusionists*. San Diego, CA: Lucent Books, 2000.

Wooten, Sara McIntosh. *Oprah Winfrey: Talk Show Legend*. Berkeley Heights, NJ: Enslow Publications, Inc., 1999.

Wordsworth, R. D., compiler. *"Abe" Lincoln's Anecdotes and Stories*. Boston, MA: The Mutual Book Company, 1908.

Wright, David K. *Arthur Ashe: Breaking the Color Barrier in Tennis*. Springfield, NJ: Enslow Publications, Inc., 1996.

Zolotow, Maurice. *No People Like Show People*. New York: Random House, 1951.

# ABOUT THE AUTHOR

It was a dark and stormy night. Suddenly a cry rang out, and on a hot summer night in 1954, Josephine, wife of Carl Bruce, gave birth to a boy—me. Unfortunately, this young married couple allowed Reuben Saturday, Josephine's brother, to name their first-born. Reuben, aka "The Joker," decided that Bruce was a nice name, so he decided to name me Bruce Bruce. I have gone by my middle name—David—ever since.

Being named Bruce David Bruce hasn't been all bad. Bank tellers remember me very quickly, so I don't often have to show an ID. It can be fun in charades, also. When I was a counselor as a teenager at Camp Echoing Hills in Warsaw, Ohio, a fellow counselor gave the signs for "sounds like" and "two words," then she pointed to a bruise on her leg twice. Bruise Bruise? Oh yeah, Bruce Bruce is the answer!

Uncle Reuben, by the way, gave me a haircut when I was in kindergarten. He cut my hair short and shaved a small bald spot on the back of my head. My mother wouldn't let me go to school until the bald spot grew out again.

Of all my brothers and sisters (six in all), I am the only transplant to Athens, Ohio. I was born in Newark, Ohio, and have lived all around Southeastern Ohio. However, I moved to Athens to go to Ohio University and have never left.

At Ohio U, I never could make up my mind whether to major in English or Philosophy, so I got a bachelor's degree with a double major in both areas, then I added a Master of Arts degree in English and a Master of Arts degree in Philosophy. Yes, I have my MAMA degree.

Currently, and for a long time to come (I eat fruits and veggies), I am spending my retirement writing books such as *Nadia Comaneci: Perfect 10*, *The Funniest People in Comedy*, *Homer's* Iliad: *A Retelling in Prose*, and *William Shakespeare's* Hamlet: *A Retelling in Prose*.

If all goes well, I will publish one or two books a year for the rest of my life. (On the other hand, a good way to make God laugh is to tell Her your plans.)

By the way, my sister Brenda Kennedy writes romances such as *A New Beginning* and *Shattered Dreams*.

# SOME BOOKS BY DAVID BRUCE

**Good Deeds**

*The Kindest People Who Do Good Deeds: Volume 1*

*The Kindest People Who Do Good Deeds: Volume 2*

**Retellings of a Classic Work of Literature**

Arden of Faversham*: A Retelling*

*Ben Jonson's* The Alchemist: *A Retelling*

*Ben Jonson's* The Arraignment, or Poetaster: *A Retelling*

*Ben Jonson's* Bartholomew Fair: *A Retelling*

*Ben Jonson's* The Case is Altered: *A Retelling*

*Ben Jonson's* Catiline's Conspiracy: *A Retelling*

*Ben Jonson's* The Devil is an Ass: *A Retelling*

*Ben Jonson's* Epicene: *A Retelling*

*Ben Jonson's* Every Man in His Humor: *A Retelling*

*Ben Jonson's* Every Man Out of His Humor: *A Retelling*

*Ben Jonson's* The Fountain of Self-Love, or Cynthia's Revels: *A Retelling*

*Ben Jonson's* The Magnetic Lady, or Humors Reconciled: *A Retelling*

*Ben Jonson's* The New Inn, or The Light Heart: *A Retelling*

*Ben Jonson's* Sejanus' Fall: *A Retelling*

*Ben Jonson's* The Staple of News: *A Retelling*

*Ben Jonson's* A Tale of a Tub: *A Retelling*

*Ben Jonson's* Volpone, or the Fox: *A Retelling*

*Christopher Marlowe's Complete Plays: Retellings*

*Christopher Marlowe's* Dido, Queen of Carthage: *A Retelling*

*Christopher Marlowe's* Doctor Faustus: *Retellings of the 1604 A-Text and of the 1616 B-Text*

*Christopher Marlowe's* Edward II: *A Retelling*

*Christopher Marlowe's* The Massacre at Paris: *A Retelling*

*Christopher Marlowe's* The Rich Jew of Malta: *A Retelling*

*Christopher Marlowe's* Tamburlaine, Parts 1 and 2: *Retellings*

*Dante's* Divine Comedy: *A Retelling in Prose*

*Dante's* Inferno: *A Retelling in Prose*

*Dante's* Purgatory: *A Retelling in Prose*

*Dante's* Paradise: *A Retelling in Prose*

The Famous Victories of Henry V: *A Retelling*

*From the* Iliad *to the* Odyssey: *A Retelling in Prose of Quintus of Smyrna's* Posthomerica

*George Chapman, Ben Jonson, and John Marston's* Eastward Ho! *A Retelling*

*George Peele's* The Arraignment of Paris: *A Retelling*

*George Peele's* The Battle of Alcazar: *A Retelling*

*George Peele's* David and Bathsheba, and the Tragedy of Absalom: *A Retelling*

*George Peele's* Edward I: *A Retelling*

*George Peele's* The Old Wives' Tale: *A Retelling*

George-a-Greene: *A Retelling*

The History of King Leir: *A Retelling*

*Homer's* Iliad: *A Retelling in Prose*

*Homer's* Odyssey: *A Retelling in Prose*

*J.W. Gent.'s* The Valiant Scot: *A Retelling*

*Jason and the Argonauts: A Retelling in Prose of Apollonius of Rhodes'* Argonautica

*John Ford: Eight Plays Translated into Modern English*

*John Ford's* The Broken Heart: *A Retelling*

*John Ford's* The Fancies, Chaste and Noble: *A Retelling*

*John Ford's* The Lady's Trial: *A Retelling*

*John Ford's* The Lover's Melancholy: *A Retelling*

*John Ford's* Love's Sacrifice: *A Retelling*

*John Ford's* Perkin Warbeck: *A Retelling*

*John Ford's* The Queen: *A Retelling*

*John Ford's* 'Tis Pity She's a Whore: *A Retelling*

*John Lyly's* Campaspe: *A Retelling*

*John Lyly's* Endymion, The Man in the Moon: *A Retelling*

*John Lyly's* Galatea: *A Retelling*

*John Lyly's* Love's Metamorphosis: *A Retelling*

*John Lyly's* Midas: *A Retelling*

*John Lyly's* Mother Bombie: *A Retelling*

*John Lyly's* Sappho and Phao: *A Retelling*

*John Lyly's* The Woman in the Moon: *A Retelling*

*John Webster's* The White Devil: *A Retelling*

King Edward III: *A Retelling*

Mankind: *A Medieval Morality Play* (A Retelling)

*Margaret Cavendish's* The Unnatural Tragedy: *A Retelling*

The Merry Devil of Edmonton: *A Retelling*

The Summoning of Everyman: *A Medieval Morality Play* (A Retelling)

*Robert Greene's* Friar Bacon and Friar Bungay: *A Retelling*

The Taming of a Shrew: *A Retelling*

*Tarlton's Jests: A Retelling*

*Thomas Middleton's* A Chaste Maid in Cheapside: *A Retelling*

*Thomas Middleton's* Women Beware Women: *A Retelling*

*Thomas Middleton and Thomas Dekker's* The Roaring Girl: *A Retelling*

*Thomas Middleton and William Rowley's* The Changeling: *A Retelling*

*The Trojan War and Its Aftermath: Four Ancient Epic Poems*

*Virgil's* Aeneid: *A Retelling in Prose*

*William Shakespeare's 5 Late Romances: Retellings in Prose*

*William Shakespeare's 10 Histories: Retellings in Prose*

*William Shakespeare's 11 Tragedies: Retellings in Prose*

*William Shakespeare's 12 Comedies: Retellings in Prose*

*William Shakespeare's 38 Plays: Retellings in Prose*

*William Shakespeare's 1 Henry IV, aka Henry IV, Part 1: A Retelling in Prose*

*William Shakespeare's 2 Henry IV, aka Henry IV, Part 2: A Retelling in Prose*

*William Shakespeare's 1 Henry VI, aka Henry VI, Part 1: A Retelling in Prose*

*William Shakespeare's 2 Henry VI, aka Henry VI, Part 2: A Retelling in Prose*

*William Shakespeare's 3 Henry VI, aka Henry VI, Part 3: A Retelling in Prose*

*William Shakespeare's All's Well that Ends Well: A Retelling in Prose*

*William Shakespeare's Antony and Cleopatra: A Retelling in Prose*

*William Shakespeare's As You Like It: A Retelling in Prose*

*William Shakespeare's The Comedy of Errors: A Retelling in Prose*

*William Shakespeare's Coriolanus: A Retelling in Prose*

*William Shakespeare's Cymbeline: A Retelling in Prose*

*William Shakespeare's Hamlet: A Retelling in Prose*

*William Shakespeare's Henry V: A Retelling in Prose*

*William Shakespeare's Henry VIII: A Retelling in Prose*

*William Shakespeare's Julius Caesar: A Retelling in Prose*

*William Shakespeare's King John: A Retelling in Prose*

*William Shakespeare's King Lear: A Retelling in Prose*

*William Shakespeare's Love's Labor's Lost: A Retelling in Prose*

*William Shakespeare's Macbeth: A Retelling in Prose*

*William Shakespeare's Measure for Measure: A Retelling in Prose*

*William Shakespeare's The Merchant of Venice: A Retelling in Prose*

*William Shakespeare's The Merry Wives of Windsor: A Retelling in Prose*

*William Shakespeare's A Midsummer Night's Dream: A Retelling in Prose*

*William Shakespeare's Much Ado About Nothing: A Retelling in Prose*

*William Shakespeare's Othello: A Retelling in Prose*

*William Shakespeare's Pericles, Prince of Tyre: A Retelling in Prose*

*William Shakespeare's Richard II: A Retelling in Prose*

*William Shakespeare's Richard III: A Retelling in Prose*

*William Shakespeare's Romeo and Juliet: A Retelling in Prose*

*William Shakespeare's The Taming of the Shrew: A Retelling in Prose*

*William Shakespeare's The Tempest: A Retelling in Prose*

*William Shakespeare's Timon of Athens: A Retelling in Prose*

*William Shakespeare's Titus Andronicus: A Retelling in Prose*

*William Shakespeare's Troilus and Cressida: A Retelling in Prose*

*William Shakespeare's Twelfth Night: A Retelling in Prose*

*William Shakespeare's The Two Gentlemen of Verona: A Retelling in Prose*

*William Shakespeare's The Two Noble Kinsmen: A Retelling in Prose*

*William Shakespeare's The Winter's Tale: A Retelling in Prose*

**Children's Biography**

*The Most Interesting People in Movies: 250 Anecdotes*
*The Most Interesting People in Politics and History: 250 Anecdotes*
*The Most Interesting People in Politics and History, Volume 2: 250 Anecdotes*
*The Most Interesting People in Politics and History, Volume 3: 250 Anecdotes*
*The Most Interesting People in Religion: 250 Anecdotes*
*The Most Interesting People in Sports: 250 Anecdotes*
*The Most Interesting People Who Live Life: 250 Anecdotes*
*The Most Interesting People Who Live Life, Volume 2: 250 Anecdotes*
*Reality is Fabulous: 250 Anecdotes and Stories*
*Resist Psychic Death: 250 Anecdotes*
*Seize the Day: 250 Anecdotes and Stories*